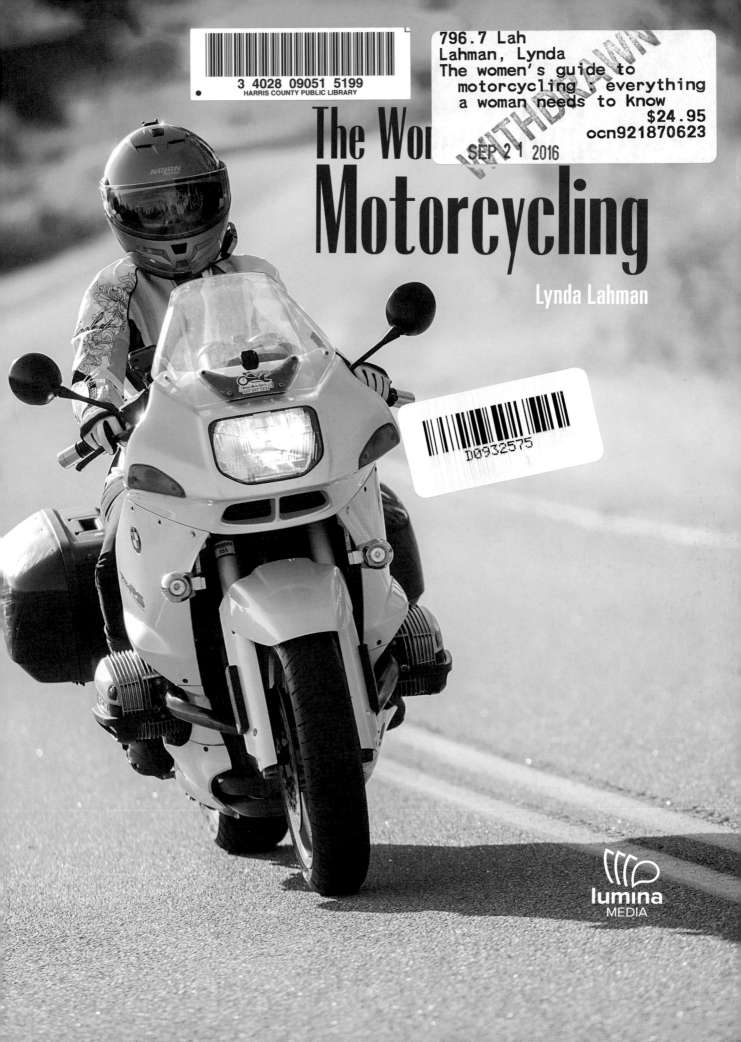

3 4028 09051 5199
HARRIS COUNTY PUBLIC LIBRARY

796.7 Lah
Lahman, Lynda
The women's guide to
motorcycling : everything
a woman needs to know
$24.95
ocn921870623

WITHDRAWN
SEP 21 2016

D0932575

The Wor
Motorcycling

Lynda Lahman

lumina
MEDIA

The Women's Guide to Motorcycling

Project Team
Editor: Amy Deputato
Copy Editor: Joann Woy
Design: Mary Ann Kahn
Index: Elizabeth Walker

LUMINA MEDIA™
Chairman: David Fry
Chief Executive Officer: Keith Walter
Chief Financial Officer: David Katzoff
Chief Digital Officer: Jennifer Black-Glover
Vice President Content: Joyce Bautista-Ferrari
Vice President Marketing & PR: Cameron Triebwasser
Managing Director, Books: Christopher Reggio
Art Director, Books: Mary Ann Kahn
Senior Editor, Books: Amy Deputato
Production Director: Laurie Panaggio
Production Manager: Jessica Jaensch

Copyright © 2016 Lumina Media, LLC™

All rights reserved. No part of this book may be reproduced, stored in a retrieval system, or transmitted in any form or by any means, electronic, mechanical, photocopying, recording, or otherwise, without the prior written permission of Lumina Media, except for the inclusion of brief quotations in an acknowledged review.

ISBN 978-1-62008-209-6

Library of Congress Cataloging-in-Publication Data has been applied for.

This book has been published with the intent to provide accurate and authoritative information in regard to the subject matter within. While every precaution has been taken in the preparation of this book, the author and publisher expressly disclaim any responsibility for any errors, omissions, or adverse effects arising from the use or application of the information contained herein.

lumina MEDIA
2030 Main Street, Suite 1400
Irvine, CA 92614
www.facebook.com/luminamediabooks
www.luminamedia.com

Printed and bound in China
19 18 17 16   2 4 6 8 10 9 7 5 3 1
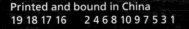

Contents

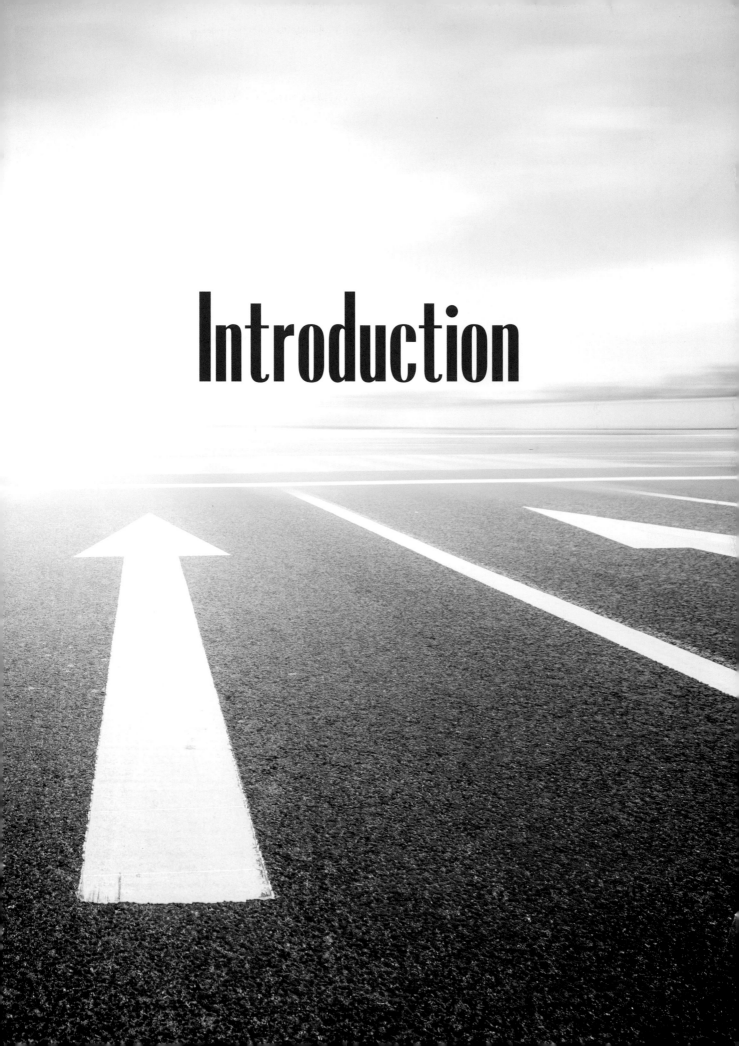

Introduction

A motorcycle doesn't know if its rider is male or female, and the techniques of riding don't change based on sex. Riding instructors describe their female students as highly attentive, willing to listen, and even able to take feedback better than their male counterparts. So why write a motorcycling book specifically for women? While there are bold, confident women who have taken up motorcycling without a second thought, more often than not, women describe a hesitation when it comes to motorcycling. The same instructors who rave about their students notice a similar trend. Women riders often struggle with speaking up for themselves once they leave the practice course, finding instead that they give in to the demands or expectations of others. Women report lower confidence in their abilities and feelings of fear or anxiety when practicing the skills necessary to build that sense of confidence. These same themes emerge when I speak with groups of women and listen to their stories of learning to ride.

What also becomes clear is that as women gain competence through practice, they find their voices. As a result, their confidence grows exponentially, and this growth isn't limited to the arena of motorcycling. Navigating U-turns, handling tight curves, and keeping the bike upright on uneven ground builds a sense of mastery for riding, and that sense of mastery carries over into many other areas of their lives. Whether they choose to ride solo, with partners, in groups of women, or with co-ed groups, once they experience the sense of personal empowerment

that comes with safely navigating the intricacies of maneuvering a motorcycle, they describe being changed in ways they never imagined. The path of self-discovery can take many unexpected twists and turns, and often a rider's journey winds up being quite different from what she first envisioned.

I started riding with a boyfriend as a pillion, or passenger. We broke up, and I missed riding. I decided it was easier to learn to ride and get a bike than to find another boyfriend, and I've been riding ever since. I've heard many variations of this story repeatedly; for example, being introduced to riding on the back of a friend's bike but realizing that it's more fun to be the one doing the driving.

I have my endorsement, but I found over time that I liked riding on the back with my husband. I don't feel the need to be as attentive to every detail, and I can enjoy practicing my photography as we ride through incredible scenery. Whether on the front seat or the rear, you are a rider. Knowing as much as possible about how the motorcycle works and wearing all the gear, all the time, makes you a better passenger even if you never start the engine on a bike and take off on your own.

I rode a motorcycle on my own for years until I had a freak accident that almost cost me my life. Once I recovered, I realized that I missed riding but wasn't sure I wanted to get back on two wheels. Finding the three-wheeled Spyder gave me back the freedom and community I missed with the level of comfort I needed. Riding is riding; being out in the elements, tackling the challenges of the twisties or on a quiet back road, is what motorcycling is about. It's not about whether you have two wheels in front, two wheels in back, or a third wheel on a sidecar, and don't listen to anyone who tells you otherwise.

This not a "how to ride" book; there are already dozens of books and hundreds of courses that will help you learn the technical aspects of riding. This book discusses what to consider when deciding whether motorcycling is for you, what steps to take if you are becoming involved, and what to do after you take your introductory courses. I hope that it provides some answers to questions you may not even know to ask before you get on your motorcycle. It addresses some of the issues I wish I had known about before I started; it might have saved me a few bruises and headaches, not to mention quite a few dollars. The information in this book is based on the collective wisdom of all of the female riders who have come before me and those who are out there riding today.

Women discuss the importance of having supporters on their journeys into the world of motorcycling. Many of those supporters were husbands, fathers, brothers, and male friends because women riders were few and far between. Today, that isn't the case: women riders are everywhere, and our numbers continue to grow. What is important is to create a network of knowledgeable and caring people who will encourage your journey to becoming a competent, confident, and safe rider. I hope that this book will be one of your first companions as you build your own support system on the road to becoming a successful motorcyclist.

Chapter 1

The Rise of Women in Motorcycling

Looking at the history of motorcycles through the years, there have always been a small number of women who have defied convention, hopped on bikes, and taken to the roads or tracks. The women's movement in the 1970s brought a few more into the fold, but female ridership remained low until the beginning of the new millennium, when it really began taking off. What is it that's bringing women in such large numbers into the world of motorcycling? The same lures that have been drawing men in for decades: it's fun, exciting, challenging, and a great way to see the world.

In fact, women have now become one of the fastest growing segments of the motorcycling market, with ridership increasing approximately 35 percent between 2003 and 2012. It is estimated that nearly a quarter of all riders in the United States are female, and new-rider educators are seeing up to half of their classes filled by these women. Harley-Davidson reports that half of all of their new-motorcycle sales are to females. Clearly, this is a trend that shows no signs of slowing.

Female riders report greater satisfaction in all areas of their lives, including greater self-confidence and increased feelings of sex appeal, than their nonriding peers, according to a 2013 study commissioned by Harley-Davidson. Almost 75 percent of the women interviewed believe that their lives have improved since they started riding. The female riders I meet support these findings: riding a motorcycle is empowering and social, and it fulfills a desire to challenge themselves. They feel competent, sexy, and engaged, and—to top it off—it's just downright fun.

The motorcycle market has finally started to take notice of the growing female presence. It's becoming easier to find a wider variety of bikes to fit smaller frames, protective gear designed to fit the female shape, and female-exclusive groups offering support and mentoring. When I first started riding, there were few options for gear, such as pants or jackets, tailored to the female figure, and not many motorcycles, other than cruiser styles or sport bikes, had a low enough seat to fit someone of a smaller stature. Manufacturers are reaching out to this new ridership, launching campaigns to draw women to their brand and hoping to establish lifetime loyalties.

A RECENT EXCHANGE ON FACEBOOK

Anthony
I have been riding for almost 30 years. Up until the past few years, it was rare to see female riders, and even rarer to see females riding solo. I used to get excited when I saw a female rider. Now it is so commonplace, it doesn't even register anymore.

Jody
Isn't it great!! I still get lots of stares and conversation, though, due to my age and white hair.

Betsy
I've been riding my own for 42 years. You can imagine growing up in the Bible Belt ... how it was frowned on by many and celebrated by others. I was an anomaly in most people's eyes, but growing up in a motorcycle family, it was my normal. I have been thrilled beyond words seeing more lady riders, riding their own bikes and having "girlfriends" that share the wanderlust. And not just riding but truly embracing the adventure, spirit, and independence that only two wheels can bring! Cheers to all the lady riders ... we celebrate you!

Royal Enfield built its first bike in 1901.
Pictured is a 1939 Royal Enfield Bullet 500cc.

Women and Motorcycling: A Brief History

There is no single moment when the motorcycle was invented; instead, its early evolution consists of various adaptations of bicycles and power until the engines outgrew the frames of the small bikes. In the early 1900s, manufacturers such as Royal Enfield, Norton, Indian, Triumph, and Harley-Davidson were producing motorcycles for the public. World War I brought an increase to the market because bikes enabled better communications to the front lines, replacing the more vulnerable and expensive-to-maintain horses.

   While men have dominated the field for years, there was a brief time in the early days of the sport when women and men alike could be found riding—before it was no longer considered feminine to hop on a bike. In the early days, when motorcycles were little more than bicycles with motors attached, they were far more affordable for the average driver than cars and were initially purchased as inexpensive forms of transportation. Families purchased bikes with sidecars, and children sat alongside their parents as they rode around town. Hill racing and motorcycle polo became favorite activities. However, the price of automobiles dropped significantly, making cars—which were an even more convenient form of transportation in a wider variety of conditions—available to the average driver. Motorcycles were no longer considered proper or ladylike, and women were soon discouraged, and often banned, from riding.

Despite the changing perception that motorcycling was now a sport primarily for men, a small number of women continued to ride. Defying social norms and often their own families, these women were the early pioneers of motorcycling, breaking down barriers and setting records while pursuing their passion. There are undoubtedly many unsung heroes among their number, but a few stand out in the history of women and riding.

One of the first women on record, Clara Wagner, who rode a 4-horsepower (hp) motorcycle, competed in and won a 365-mile endurance race from Chicago to Indianapolis in 1910, only to be denied her trophy. The reason? She was ruled "an unofficial entrant" due to being female.

Della Crewe, navigating her Harley-Davidson with a sidecar nicknamed "The Gray Fellow" that carried her dog, Trouble, left Waco, Texas, in June of 1914 for a grand tour. Arriving in New York City in December 1914, reportedly wearing four coats, four pairs of stockings, and heavy sheepskin shoes, Crewe eventually covered more than 11,000 miles through North and South America before fading into obscurity.

The first women known publicly to cross the United States on a motorcycle were the mother–daughter duo of twenty-six-year-old Effie Hotchkiss and her fifty-six-year-old mother, Avis. Bored with her job, eager for a chance to see the country, and fascinated by two-wheeled motorized machines, Effie was often described as a tomboy and a speed demon. Avis's motivation was somewhat different from her daughter's: she went along more to keep Effie out of trouble than out of any desire to travel. Efforts to discourage their journey with tales of potential dangers along the way only further piqued Effie's interest and determination. Riding a three-speed V-twin Harley-Davidson with a sidecar, which, in the words of Effie, was best suited "for myself, and the sidecar for my mother and the luggage," the women left Brooklyn, New York, on May 2, 1915. Forty years before the interstate highway system was even signed into law, they faced "bad roads, heat, cold, rain, floods, and all such things with a shrug of their shoulders" as described in the September 1915 issue of *Harley-Davidson Dealer* magazine. Tracing a route that took them from upstate New York through Chicago, south to St. Louis, east through Kansas and Colorado, south again to Santa Fe, and then on to Arizona, they reached Los Angeles and the Pacific Ocean in August. Returning home, they took a more northerly route, passing through San Francisco, Reno, Salt Lake City, Wyoming, Nebraska, and Iowa before stopping in Milwaukee for a tour of the Harley-Davidson factory. They arrived safely back in Brooklyn in October of the same year. Effie's motorcycling days soon came to an end when she married a widower she had met along her ride and relocated with her mother to pursue a different sort of adventure in rural Oregon.

The following year, Augusta and Adeline Van Buren, American sisters in their twenties who had hoped to be allowed to become military dispatch riders during World War I, set off on a cross-country trek to demonstrate their skills and determination. Riding separate Indian Power Plus motorcycles and believing, as Augusta stated, "women can if they will," they started their ride in Sheepshead Bay, New York, on July 2, 1916. Traversing the United States, they were arrested in a small town west of Chicago— not for speeding, but for wearing men's clothes. Arguing that their leather apparel was more appropriate for motorcycling than were dresses, they were able to convince the authorities to let them proceed.

A Harley-Davidson Electra Glide Ultra Classic with sidecar on display at an "oldtimers' show" in Germany.

Continuing on, they became the first women to summit Pike's Peak in Colorado, an elevation of 14,109 feet up a narrow, dangerous dirt road. Battling fatigue, heat, poor roads, and numerous falls, they arrived in Los Angeles on September 8. To ensure that they were credited for traversing the entire country, they rode to Tijuana, Mexico, before returning home. Articles written about their adventure eloquently described their motorcycles but dismissed the sisters' efforts as merely a vacation. Despite their accomplishment of being the first women to complete a transcontinental journey, proving that they were equal to their male

Crystal Palace Park in London was a well known motorcycle-racing venue in pre-World War II days.

counterparts, their applications to become dispatch riders were rejected. However, demonstrating their pioneering spirit in the face of obstacles, Adeline went on to earn a law degree from New York University while Augusta learned to fly, becoming a pilot in the 99s, a group for women flyers founded in 1929 by Amelia Earhart.

An Irish motorcyclist, Fay Taylour, bought a helmet and took up riding so that she "could mingle with the English boys at the next Crystal Palace practice session." The Palace was one of the first dirt-track racing facilities built in England after the sport was introduced from Australia. Nicknamed "Flying Fay," she began competing in grass-track racing and motorcycle trials as well as the World Speedway events in the late 1920s and early 1930s.

Two of Taylour's most celebrated contemporaries were Dot Dawson and Marjorie Cottle. Cottle, one of the most well-known motorcyclists of her time, is perhaps best remembered for riding around the coast of mainland Britain in 1924 as part of an advertising stunt staged by the Raleigh company to promote the suitability of riding for women. A male rider, Hugh Gibson, riding a 7-hp Raleigh with a sidecar, took off in one direction while Cottle, on a 2¾-hp Raleigh Solo, took off at the same time in the opposite direction. The company took bets as to where they'd meet, and between 60,000 and 70,000 people participated, each one hoping to win a motorcycle for guessing the correct location. Cottle was quoted as saying, "Completed 3,404 miles around the coast of Great Britain … and have shown that what man has done woman can do … I hope that I have proven, that with a Raleigh, touring a motor-cycle [sic] is a woman's pastime, and I hope the women of Britain will follow my example," in the *Western Daily Press* on June 12, 1924.

Women were banned from road racing in Britain in 1925, but that didn't stop them from competing in races. Along with Louise Maclean and Edyth Foley, Cottle went on to compete in the International Six Days Trials, an off-road endurance event started in Britain in 1913; she finished in the Silver Vase category in 1926 and bested all others, including the men's teams, to win the top honors in 1927.

Other than Raleigh in England, Harley-Davidson in the United States was one of the few manufacturers to encourage women to ride. Always on the lookout for new sales opportunities, dealers were reminded to look at their wives and daughters as potential customers. Vivian Bales, riding from Georgia to Milwaukee and back in 1929, a distance of 5,000 miles, began billing herself, to the delight of the company, as "The Enthusiast Girl" after photos of her appeared in the *Harley-Davidson Enthusiast* magazine.

Theresa Wallach, born and raised near the English factories of Norton, BSA, and Triumph motorcycles, learned to ride from her many friends who worked at the plants. Refused membership in a local riding club due to her sex, she proved her racing skills by competing in, and winning, numerous events. She and another accomplished woman motorcyclist, Florence Blenkiron, set off in 1935 to ride from London to Cape Town, South Africa, on a 650cc Panther, complete with a sidecar and towing a utility trailer. No one, male or female, had attempted such a journey. Taking turns driving, often pushing or dragging the bike along on foot when it became stuck, they traveled across the Sahara Desert, following rock outcroppings and guideposts set up for caravans because building roads was impossible in the drifting sands. Fighting heat, torrential rains, mechanical breakdowns, dealings with the French Foreign Legion, and wild animals, they miraculously arrived safely after seven months of travel. Wallach chronicled their journey in the book *The Rugged Road*, which is still available today. While Blenkiron disappeared into oblivion following her return to England, Wallach

A vintage Triumph Coventry motorcycle.

A vintage British Army motorcycle made by Royal Enfield.

continued to make history, becoming the first woman to win the Brooklands Gold Star in 1939 for setting a world record by topping 100 miles per hour on a borrowed single-cylinder Norton 350cc.

It wasn't until World War II that women were allowed to join the ranks of dispatch riders, and Wallach signed up, working with the British Army as both a motorcycle mechanic and dispatch rider. Always dreaming of a trip to America, following the war, she spent two and a half years traversing the country, camping and working odd jobs to fund her travels. She fell in love with the United States and emigrated, settling first in Chicago, where she opened a dealership called Imported Motorcycles, Inc., which specialized in selling and servicing British motorcycles. She noticed the inexperience of many new riders, so she began

> "When I first saw a motorcycle, I got a message from it. It was a feeling—the kind of thing that makes a person burst into tears [upon] hearing a piece of music or standing awestruck in front of a fine work of art. Motorcycling is a tool with which you can accomplish something meaningful in your life. It is an art."
>
> —Theresa Wallach, *Road Rider Magazine*, 1977

teaching them basic riding techniques. Realizing the need for better instruction, she sold her dealership and moved to Phoenix, Arizona, where she launched the Easy Riding Academy. In 1970, her book, *Easy Motorcycle Riding*, was published.

Born to a motorcycling family in Australia in 1912, Dot Robinson's first ride was in a sidecar, when her father drove her mother to the hospital for her delivery. Her exposure to bikes continued when the family moved to the United States when she was still a child. Growing up in her father's motorcycle dealership, she learned to ride at a young age and was competing in endurance races during the 1930s, '40s, and '50s despite pressure from others to stop. She won her first trophy in 1930 in the Flint 100, and she went on to enter the Jack Pine Enduro in 1934, continuing to enter this competition in subsequent years. An off-road competition, the Jack Pine sent riders through every type of terrain imaginable while requiring them to meet certain time limitations at checkpoints. It was originally a three-day 800 miler but was reduced to two days and 500 miles. In its early years, the Jack Pine Enduro was as popular as the prestigious Daytona 200 and Laconia motorcycle races. Robinson was the first woman to win this prestigious race, doing so in 1940 in the sidecar division, and she repeated her accomplishment in 1946. Often called the "First Lady of Motorcycling," Robinson's dedication to endurance riding opened the doors for many of the women who followed.

Following in the footsteps of female pioneers, women riders continue to do remarkable things.

Robinson, along with her friend Linda Dugeau, a touring motorcyclist who often appeared in the pages of *Motorcyclist* magazine, wanted to create a network of riders by forming an organization devoted exclusively to women. The two began a letter-writing campaign in 1938, reaching out to dealerships, American Motorcyclist Association (AMA) members, and fellow riders, hoping to find like-minded enthusiasts. It took three years to round up enough interest to start, and Motor Maids was chartered through the AMA in 1941. It was the first motorcycling organization for women in the United States.

Louise Scherbyn spent her early years riding both as pillion, or passenger, and in a sidecar until 1932, when her husband encouraged her to teach herself to

ride. Initially concerned with her reputation, especially the impact on her job at Kodak, she soon shed her reluctance and began traveling extensively throughout the United States and Canada. Scherbyn went on to become a full-time writer and assistant editor for *Motorcycle* magazine, where she used her talent to continue breaking stereotypes, promoting and encouraging the acceptance of women riders in a field dominated by men.

Becoming active in motorcycling clubs, Scherbyn corresponded with women across the globe. It was through these connections that she formed the idea of creating the Women's International Motorcycle Association (WIMA), which was born in the early 1950s, with Theresa Wallach as its first vice president. Enlisting the support of other notable women riders, including Anke-Eve Goldman and Ellen Pfeiffer in Germany, Agnes Acker in France, Juliette Steiner in Switzerland, Lydia Abrahamova in Czechoslovakia (now the Czech Republic), and Hazel Mayes in Australia, WIMA expanded beyond the United States to Europe and then throughout the world.

Adding to the challenge of gender barriers, Bessie Stringfield faced racial barriers as well when she began riding at the age of sixteen. A petite African American woman, she pursued her passion for motorcycling; at age nineteen, she started tossing pennies on a map to determine where to head on her next trip. Encountering the rampant racism of her time, she was once run off the road by a white man in a pick-up truck but refused to be discouraged, relying on her strong faith as her companion. Working as a dispatch rider during World War II, the only woman in her unit, she carried documents between bases throughout the

"Years ago, the doctor wanted to stop me from riding," she recalled, because she suffered from an enlarged heart. "I told him if I don't ride, I won't live long. And so I never did quit."
—Bessie Stringfield

United States. She completed eight solo cross-country trips before settling down in Miami, Florida, in the 1950s. She became a licensed practical nurse and continued riding—competing in hill climbs, performing motorcycle stunts in carnival shows, and founding the Iron Horse Motorcycle Club. Known as the "Motorcycle Queen of Miami," Stringfield was honored with the American Motorcycle Association's creation of the Bessie Stringfield Award in 2000, recognizing "women who have been instrumental in showing women they can be active participants in the world of motorcycling."

The popularity of motorcycling among women began to increase following World War II, coinciding with their changing roles at home and in the workforce. Margaret Wilson was one of the role models for these new times. She and her husband, Mike, were the owners of Wilson's Motorcycle Sales in Cedar Rapids, Iowa, and it was Mike who taught her to ride in 1946. Joining Motor Maids in 1951, she put more than 550,000 miles on her bikes and performed on her club's drill team while being among the first riders to promote the wearing of helmets and protective clothing. She was voted "America's Most Popular" and "Typical Girl Rider" for 1958 by the AMA, and she served on the founding board of the AMA Hall of Fame Museum. She was inducted into the Sturgis Motorcycle Hall

Cletha Walstrom conquered the Abra Malaga mountain pass in Macchu Picchu, Peru, in 2013.

> *"At a party, car racer Steve McQueen said, 'McGee, you've got to get off that road-racing bike and come out to the desert.' I told him that I didn't want to get dirty, but I did say it might be fun. My husband worked for Honda, so a 250 Honda Scrambler was my ride. Dirt bikes were to stay in my future, including desert, motocross, and the long-distance races. My career highlight racing bikes in Baja was in 1975, when I rode a 250 Husqvarna solo in the Baja 500, passing seventeen two-man teams. The hardest thing I ever did was Baja. It was very barren: no electricity, no doctors, no phone. I carried Percodan in case of injury because you'd have to ride injured to get to someplace where someone has a car to get to Ensenada or La Paz to a clinic or back to the States. Luckily, I never had to use the Percodan, but I did come off the bike several times."*
>
> —Mary McGee, *Motorcycle Mojo*, April 2013

of Fame in 2011. Wilson passed away on July 23, 2014, at the age of ninety-eight, an active supporter of all riders—especially women—until her death.

Mary McGee began road-racing motorcycles in 1960 and was the first woman licensed by the Fédération Internationale de Motocyclisme (FIM). She became the first female to compete in motocross in 1967, and she entered the inaugural Baja 500 in 1969, teamed with a male rider. Their bike failed, but she came back to finish as part of a team in 1973 and solo in 1975. In 2012, at the age of seventy-five, she was still competing in vintage-class motorcycle races.

The International Six Days Trial continued to attract an increasing number of women as it branched out from Britain and began holding competitions in other countries. Notable rider Olga Kevelos, winner of two gold medals—one in 1946 and again in 1953—was offered a sponsorship from the James Motorcycle Company, an honor almost unheard of for a woman in her day. Other manufacturers quickly added their names to her list of supporters as she went on to compete until her retirement from the sport in 1970.

Into the Twenty-First Century

Overall motorcycle ridership declined during the 1950s and '60s before experiencing a resurgence in the 1970s, when it became part of a growing leisure-time pursuit. Improved machines, the emergence of the Japanese motorcycling industry, the rise of the sport bikes from Italy, and the reliable BMW twins from Germany all contributed to the excitement and popularity of riding. More women were entering the field of motorcycling alongside their male counterparts, although not yet in the numbers seen today.

As the ranks of motorcyclists once again began to swell, new opportunities for competition arose as well. Increasing numbers of riders were soon choosing to go out not only for pleasure trips but also to race, on or off-road, against a group or against the clock, up hills or through obstacles, or in long-distance scavenger hunts called rallies. Each new avenue provided places for women to make their impact.

Motorcycle trials, or observed trials, are nonracing events over obstacle courses. The rider is scored by how many times her feet touch the ground, testing her ability and skill in maneuvering the bike in a challenging environment. A modern pioneer in trials competition, Debbie Evans began riding at age six, growing up surrounded by motorcycles and racing. Winning a third-place trophy in her first trial at age nine, she continued to pursue her passion, earning the respect of male riders with her skills. Sponsorship from Yamaha soon followed, and Evans expanded her repertoire to include performing stunts in exhibitions and shows.

People encouraged her to compete in the Scottish Six Day Trials, despite having never competed in such an event, and she finished a respectable fourth in the 175cc division. Needing to earn a living, she turned to Hollywood and became a highly sought-after stunt rider. After retiring from racing in 1980, she was tempted back to the Women's World Trials in 1998, at the age of forty, and finished eighth overall. She continued to compete and entered, although did not win, her first road-racing event at Daytona in 2002.

BMW bikes have long been known for reliability and performance. This vintage model is exhibited at the BMW Museum in Munich.

Women's motocross, combining the trials style of riding over obstacles with racing against other competitors, traces its beginnings to the 1940s, but it really took off in the 1970s as racetracks and arenas were pressured to open their doors, and riders flowed in. The first Powder Puff National Championship, an all-women's motocross competition, was held in 1974. Quickly renamed the Women's National Championship, it was televised for the first time by ABC Sports in 1979. Sue Fish was one of the first females to compete not only in the women's events but also in the Men's Pro MX, and she soon was winning against her male counterparts. Fish was honored for her achievements at the Legends and Heroes Tour on February 13, 2010, and she is the only woman motocross rider to be inducted into the AMA's Motorcycle Hall of Fame.

A female rider competes in a motocross event in Thailand.

Ashley Fiolek earned a full factory sponsorship after becoming the first deaf Women's Motocross (WMX) National Champion. She went on to win three more national championships before leaving the sport in 2012. Among the women who have followed in the footsteps of Evans, Fish, and Fiolek, Tarah Geiger won the silver medal at the X Games in 2010 and 2011.

Requiring lightning-fast reflexes and a sense of calmness to deal with the lack of traction and any sudden changes in conditions, Leslie Porterfield reached a top speed of 232.522 mph while setting the Guinness World Record for being the fastest woman on a motorcycle. Named the AMA's Racing Female Rider of the Year in 2008, Porterfield accomplished her feat at the Bonneville Salt Flats in 2008 on her 2002 2000cc turbo-charged Suzuki Hayabusa.

Valerie Thompson is often referred to as "America's Queen of Speed." Soon after learning to ride, she recognized her love of going as fast as possible on a motorcycle and began drag racing on a track. Her passion for speed led her to explore her limits at places like the Bonneville Salt Flats and El Mirage, a dry lake bed, where she competes against both men and women. She currently holds seven

> *"Racing's a very personal thing, almost a spiritual thing. It really takes a lot of personal awareness to set the record. It takes a lot of patience, a lot of focus and prep to be able to go that fast. It's definitely not a sport for everyone, and it's definitely not all machine."*
>
> —Leslie Porterfield, *Time* magazine

motorcycle land-speed records with a personal best time of 217.7 mph for the 1-mile distance.

Evolving from the earlier hill-climbing events, in which riders challenged each other to reach the top of a hill, modern-day hill climbing has entrants racing up extremely steep dirt courses, trying to make it not only without falling but also in the fastest time. With races lasting no more than several seconds, riders must use quick reflexes to navigate obstacles. Cathy Templeton is one of the earliest women to break down the gender barriers in the sport of hill climbing, beating forty-five other riders to win in her class in 1995. Contemporary hill climbers include Chelsea Peterson, who won the women's championship in 2012, and Molly Carbon, who races head-to-head against men on some of the most challenging inclines in the United States.

Traditional racing is also attracting its share of highly competitive and successful women. Elena Myers, only eighteen years old at the time, became the first female to win a professional race at the famous Daytona International Speedway in 2012. Shelina Moreda is the first woman to have raced a motorcycle at the Indianapolis Motor Speedway as well as the only woman to race in the AMA Pro Harley class. Her all-female skills course, Girlz MotoCamps, is helping to bring more young women into racing while training them to be all-around better riders.

The Iron Butt Association, an organization dedicated to safe long-distance motorcycling, requires a rider to complete a minimum ride of 1,000 miles in twenty-four hours to gain entry. In addition to specific certified rides, the association, along with other groups, holds competitive rallies that are similar to scavenger hunts. Male and female riders, as well as two-up couples, go head to head against each other. Suzie Mann was the first woman to ride in the eleven-day Iron Butt Rally in 1985, finishing in fifth place, and while a woman has yet to claim first place, Fran Crane finished second in 1987. In 2013, Wendy Crockett placed third, averaging 1,363 miles per day during the rally, which was only 43 fewer daily miles than the first-place rider. Kate Johnston, in only her third year as a motorcyclist and a type 1 diabetic, recently set the woman's world record for riding from Key West, Florida, to Prudhoe Bay, Alaska, and back to Key West in twenty-four days.

El Mirage in California's Mojave Desert.

Women are making their mark on traditional motorcycle racing.

There are women who ride around their countries, their continents, and the world solo, known only to their friends and perhaps followers of their blogs. These women quietly navigate language barriers, challenging paved and dirt roads in their efforts to see the world in a unique and up-close way. Most report feeling quite safe; in fact, they often feel more comfortable alone on their bikes than walking city streets alone. They experience most people as open and helpful to a woman alone, and they often form friendships through unexpected encounters with strangers.

Gloria Tramontin Struck, eighty-nine at the time of this writing, has been on motorcycles, always Harley-Davidsons or Indians, since she was a young girl. Putting more than 650,000 miles on her stock bikes, Struck is one of the longest riding members of Motor Maids and credits motorcycling with keeping her mind strong.

Voni Glaves and Ardys Kellerman became the first two women in the world to document 1,000,000 miles on BMW motorcycles, and they chose to celebrate their accomplishment by meeting in Ouray, Colorado, on August 30, 2011, to ride their final miles together. Glaves, who was sixty-four at the time, learned to ride on a dirt bike before receiving her first BMW as a Mother's Day present in 1977. She finished the Iron Butt Rally in 2003. Kellerman, seventy-nine at the time, bought her first BMW in 1985. In 2006, she rode more than 80,000 miles in the six-month BMW owners' mileage contest, and she finished that year with more than 100,000 miles. Kellerman only began riding in her fifties, but once she started, she kept going, completing the eleven-day Iron Butt Rally four times before her untimely death at age eighty-one in 2014.

The list goes on. Drag racing, freestyle, dirt track, ice racing, and sidecar and vintage motorcycle classes, as well as the world-renowned Paris–Dakar Rally and the Baja 1000, are attracting women in increasing numbers. For those interested in learning more about these contemporary trendsetting women, check out the detailed profiles in *Bikerlady: Living and Riding Free*, a book by Sasha Mullins (Citadel, 2003).

"You have to concentrate on what you're doing. You have to concentrate on what everybody else is doing. You have to have your eyes behind you, on the side of you, in front of you."
—Gloria Tramontin Struck, *Inside Jersey*, March 16, 2015

Although the numerous competitive events may be thrilling, the majority of women riding today are simply hopping on a bike, as either driver or pillion, and getting out on the open road. Talk to most of them, and they speak in nearly reverential terms about the experience of two wheels, of the freedom and exhilaration of being on a motorcycle, of the desire to keep going. What is it about this particular machine that captures one's imagination and makes one yearn to take off—and is it for you?

Ardys Kellerman (left) and Voni Glaves (right), at the conclusion of their 1,000,000-mile achievement.

Chapter 2

Why We Ride

From Pillion to Driver: My Story

I met my husband through the Internet, on Match.com. In his profile, he mentioned his love of motorcycling, and it seemed to be an important aspect of his recreational life. When we met in person, he talked about his passion for long-distance riding and mentioned that he commuted to work daily on his bike. When we walked out to the parking garage after a lovely dinner, we chatted next to his motorcycle while he put on his protective gear. A keen observer, I quickly put two and two together and acknowledged that he hadn't been kidding about how much he liked riding. As a therapist who had spent years working with individuals who believed that their partners would change over time, only to be bitterly disappointed when they turned out to be exactly who they said they were

at the start, I thought that it might be a good idea to see if I liked riding enough for us to continue getting to know each other further. I already enjoyed his company and was starting to develop feelings for him, but if I didn't care for motorcycling, I knew it would create problems down the road for any potential relationship.

We both expressed a desire for a partner with whom we could share a majority of our free-time activities; neither of us had a desire to be with someone whose interests didn't substantially overlap our own.

If it turned out that I didn't like motorcycles, I could easily imagine a scenario in which he'd be asking me to go for a ride, and I'd be making excuses as to why he should head out alone—a situation neither of us wanted. I'd been on a friend's bike at fifteen, and he'd taught me the basics of riding as we goofed off up and down our neighborhood streets without my parents' knowledge. I'd definitely enjoyed it, but that was many years ago!

At my request, on our third date, I borrowed some of Terry's protective gear, which was a bit too large and a bit too bulky, and he took me for an 80-mile ride through the local countryside. When we stopped for gas, he asked me how I was doing, and I couldn't get the grin off my face. Despite any discomfort from the heavy jacket and pants, I was falling in love—at that moment with the bike, and later with him. The combination of being outside and in motion; being enveloped by sights, sounds, and smells; and sharing the experience with someone whose company I was growing to enjoy was overwhelming. I was absolutely certain on that first ride that motorcycling would never be an issue that would come between us.

The father-daughter pair of Pat Ford and Rebecca Martinez ride two-up in the 2013 Iron Butt Rally.

Three months later, I was introduced to long-distance riding when Terry invited me to join him at the end of a competitive rally in Utah in which he was scheduled to participate. As he described it, these rallies were essentially scavenger hunts: riding to various locations to take pictures or answer questions to prove you'd been there. The challenge lay in solving the puzzle of which locations would earn a rider the most points during the limited time of the event. It wasn't a race, but a measure of efficiency: how quickly you could create a route and how quickly you could stop for gas and food so that you spent the majority of your time riding.

Terry had been in a rally while we were first dating, but I didn't really understand what it was or what it entailed. Our initial discussion was about whether it was worth the cost of airfare for me to fly out and meet him at the end of the rally. But my curiosity about the event turned our conversation from the logistics of travel to the purpose of rallies and why he competed in long-distance events. Before long, I broached the idea of riding the rally together, and he was open to the suggestion despite our only having taken two relatively short excursions since that first ride on our third date.

To be sure I could withstand the rigors of a twenty-six hour ride, Terry insisted that we first complete a SaddleSore ride, which is 1,000 miles in twenty-four hours. The SaddleSore is the minimum qualification for membership in the Iron Butt Association and therefore a benchmark that Terry felt was appropriate for determining my stamina. Because he was leaving the following Wednesday evening for Utah, we had to do the 1,000-mile test that weekend, only two days away. My competitive juices whetted, and not fully understanding what I was about to embark on, I naively accepted the challenge.

The SaddleSore was quite an adventure. We were almost derailed soon after we got started when someone knocked over our bike while it was parked, causing damage to the windscreen and a one-hour delay. I was heartbroken that we might have to abandon our quest and then elated when we were able to temporarily solve the problem with duct tape. Parts of the ride were brutal, and at two in the morning, when Terry needed a short nap, I was torn between gratitude and irritation. I wanted off the bike, but I was also determined to complete our quest. I quickly forgot about all of the pain, however, when we arrived back at our starting location with only twenty minutes to spare. The feeling of accomplishment was incredible, and I was surprised at what we had been able to do in only twenty-four hours.

As we were getting ready for Utah, Terry handed me a tiny canvas sack. He told me that I could pack whatever I needed for our five-day trip as long as it fit inside the bag, thus introducing me to the world of motorcycling beauty: no frills, no hair dryers, one pair of pants, a clean shirt, a bare minimum of undergarments, a toothbrush, and a wee bit of makeup. Realizing that complaining wouldn't change anything, I packed my bag, hopped on the back seat, and rode 850 miles to Salt Lake City. It was my first introduction to a large group of other motorcyclists, and they welcomed me warmly, although many questioned my sanity.

Competing in the rally was again more fun and more brutal than I had expected. Looking for bonus locations broke up the long hours, and it was thrilling when we found what we were looking for and added up our points, but the 1,245 miles in the twenty-six hours of the scavenger hunt killed my tailbone. Counting the return ride to Seattle, I had been on the pillion seat of Terry's bike for a total of nearly 4,000 miles in essentially four days of riding. Despite moments

Riding solo means more room for baggage!

of sheer exhaustion and times of pure physical agony, I loved being on the bike, being with Terry, and solving the puzzle that was rallying. Before we had even arrived home, I was plotting ways in which we could improve our performance, and we were soon entering other rallies. The following year, however, acknowledging that the bike we both loved was also the one torturing my back, I had to tell Terry that I just couldn't handle sitting for our long rides. I felt guilty because I knew what the bike meant to him, but had I kept quiet, it would have hurt our relationship even more than my tailbone. We traded for one that better fit both of our needs.

The author with her first bike.

Although I enjoyed being a passenger, I began to feel pressure, mostly internally and definitely not from Terry, to ride solo. Other women motorcyclists asked when I was going to get my own bike, and, when I hesitated, they reassured me that I would do just fine. I knew I would as well, but I wasn't sure that it was what I wanted yet. Giving in to the expectations of others, I took the Motorcycle Safety Foundation's Basic Rider Course and passed easily, obtaining my endorsement. I definitely had fun in the class and was excited to start riding.

Taking the next logical step, I quickly purchased a new bike—a bike that was entirely wrong for me. I didn't listen to my own intuition, which was telling me to get the starter bike; instead, I bought one that might be right for me in the long term but was scaring me short term. I soon found myself making excuses to avoid going out, and my enthusiasm for solo riding waned. Entering and being selected to ride two-up in the eleven-day, 11,000-mile Iron Butt Rally in 2007 gave me the perfect out: we needed to train together rather than separately. I sold my bike and returned to the role of pillion, where I happily rode for the next couple of years.

My contentment with the passenger seat lasted until Terry and I stopped competing in 2009 and began riding for fun and taking longer recreational trips. We were still covering long distances, but I found myself fighting boredom, looking forward to getting where we were going rather than eagerly anticipating the riding itself. I realized I liked being engaged; when we were in rallies, we worked intensely as a team, planning and navigating routes in our attempts to earn as many points as possible. My role was active and as important as Terry's, and I loved our interaction. Once we decided to stop competing and instead began to ride more for leisure, my role disappeared, and I found that I didn't enjoy simply sightseeing. I needed a challenge—it was time to get back on my own bike.

I had not fully appreciated that riding more than 120,000 miles as pillion would give me as many skills to draw on as a driver as it did. Having sat through

Practice makes perfect when it comes to any new endeavor in motorcycling.

long days of intense rain, having been nearly blown off the road by crosswinds, and having felt the "pucker moments," when the bike slid unexpectedly on slick painted markings on the street, I knew intuitively what the bike would and wouldn't do. I knew how it handled in a wide variety of circumstances and how it reacted when things changed suddenly. Our competitions and long hours on the road taught me how my husband thinks and responds to different situations that might arise, and I, without planning or practice, had internalized many of those same ways of riding.

I did, however, spend a lot of time practicing once I again started riding solo. I was more comfortable at speed than in tight, low-speed maneuvers. I dropped my bike several times and evaluated each mistake to figure out what I needed to be doing differently. I had to relearn just exactly how far to move my head when making a turn and how still I needed to keep it when pulling up to a gas pump. The more I rode and the more I practiced the things that scared me the most, the more my confidence grew. What I wanted to avoid early on became simple over time, and, with each ride, my excitement to get on the bike and go increased. I continue to love getting out on the motorcycle with Terry, but next to him, not behind him.

After years of riding solo, I have no desire to return to the pillion seat. I love the sense of competence that I have in solving problems on my own, and I get a much nicer view of the road without Terry's helmet in front of me. I can carry more gear, including a wider variety of clothes, and we can take camping trips that are not possible with just one bike. I now go out alone, with my husband and with girlfriends. I plan day, overnight, and even month-long trips, poring over maps and researching local motorcycle roads wherever we might be going. I love learning about destinations off the beaten track and discovering little gems missed by many who are in a hurry to get wherever they are going. My desire for adventure, challenge, and travel is fulfilled through all aspects of motorcycling, and I am completely engaged every moment that I am on the bike.

I competed solo in the 2015 Iron Butt Rally, the eleven-day, 11,000-mile long-distance scavenger hunt that we had completed twice before two-up. While I was riding, I spent time pondering the difference between pillion and driver and what it was that intrigued me about solo versus two-up motorcycling. I thought about moments in other activities where I'd felt similar sensations. Skiing came to mind, imagining the perfect run in which I would glide effortlessly down the slope, turning without thought. I thought about bicycling downhill around curves, letting the bike sway from side to side as it cornered. I thought about dancing, when the movements are seamless and everything comes together perfectly. The common theme is movement without effort, where it all plays out without trying, where I become one with what I am doing. In those moments, I am one with the motorcycle, gliding through turns, moving back and forth in rhythm, and completely in the present. No worries, no cares, no thoughts of chores needing to be done or stressors awaiting me upon my return home. I have to be focused on what I am doing, yet the focus comes easily, effortlessly. As pillion, I was part of the dance, but as the driver, I am the creator of the dance. Both have their merits, but for me, the greatest magic comes from the creation. What I also realized is that the more skillful I am as a driver, the more of those moments I am able to experience. The reason for practicing and improving is not simply to prevent accidents but to fully embrace the magic of riding.

Motorcycling fills my senses and demands my respect. In busy cities, I have to be completely focused, reading everything going on around me and anticipating things that might occur suddenly. There's no room for the minutia of everyday life, no worries about what to make for dinner or bills I need to pay. There's no email to check or texts to which I must respond. I have to stay in the moment, and, by doing so, I get a break from day-to-day demands. As several riders have described it, "When I put on my helmet, I can leave my worries behind; it's where I go for my personal space."

The intensity required to focus is surprisingly relaxing because there's nowhere else to be. I've noticed that while there are times when my mind wanders and I find myself composing stories, pondering problems, and figuring out solutions, it's a quiet background process, and my eyes and brain are still focused on the road ahead. It's as if I am thinking without thinking, putting issues on the back burner to let them percolate while I attend to the immediate task of riding,

Lynda checks in at the 2015 Iron Butt Rally, her first time doing the rally solo.

allowing my thoughts to proceed without restriction and opening my mind to solutions not otherwise possible. Quieting the electronics and unplugging from the world gives my brain the chance to take a breather, and I welcome the solitude.

With no walls around me, I am part of the landscape. From my very first ride with Terry, I found myself absorbed in my surroundings, fully immersed in the sights and smells as we rode through and past them. It's what I fell in love with in those early miles and what I still love today. I feel more intimately connected to where I am, and I take the time to genuinely experience the small towns and everyday life that, in a car, I would merely pass through, worrying more about the destination than the journey. I am continually amazed at how wonderful it is to breathe in freshly mowed grass or to know the moist aroma of a road that has recently been dampened by a brief rain shower. Driving slowly along half-deserted streets, I get whiffs of freshly baked breads or find myself suddenly desiring the mouth-watering barbecue we just passed. I can look anywhere and find something to engage me momentarily, yet the demand to look where I am heading pulls me back into the here and now, forcing me to let go and move on. Watching a sunset in its full panoramic glory while rolling through a deserted landscape, seeing the changing shapes and colors, and feeling the heat of the day slowly give way to the cooler night air cannot be replicated within the confines of a car. Motorcycling is great practice for life, learning to simply be in the moment, let go, and move on.

I have a passion for travel and a love of meeting people in their worlds. Riding a motorcycle fulfills both of those passions. Strangers come up to me, interested in seeing a female on a bike, and share their stories. Others describe the same thing: that, as women, we are somehow easier to approach, and their curiosity overrides any hesitation they may have in interrupting what we are doing. I, too, feel more

When the helmet goes on, the outside world goes away.

comfortable initiating conversations with locals at gas stations, fast-food joints, and local diners, answering their unspoken questions and often ending up in lively discussions. Chats meander from where I've been or where I'm going to what life is like in whatever town I'm passing through. I've been invited to meals by folks who would never approach me if I were in a car, and I've made lasting friendships with other riders who merely happened to be in the campsite next to mine, with initial introductions made through discussions about how we each liked the bikes we are riding. Casual relationships with motorcycling acquaintances that may have needed a place to spend the night while passing through my town have deepened into meaningful friendships after they've parked their bikes and we've shared stories over a few beers. Would they have thought to stay with me otherwise? I doubt it; motorcycling was our common ground, and that shared interest made it both easier for them to ask for and me to offer a bed for the night.

I've ridden the entire United States in the span of eight days, experiencing the different regions within a very short time. The thought of doing that in a car sounds horrid, but on the bike, it was wonderful to experience the country through all of my senses. I've been on incredible back roads that I'd never have known about or ventured off onto except when lured by reviews from other motorcycle enthusiasts. Riding late at night in the middle of nowhere, I've found myself mesmerized by the array of stars overhead, untouched by the light pollution from the cities. Needing to absorb it all, I've sometimes pulled over by the side of the road just to get off the bike and soak it all in. Over the years, I've gone with others on memorial rides to remember motorcycling friends we've lost, sharing our grief and telling stories to help us laugh again. And while it may sound insane to some, I've ridden hundreds of miles to join others for a hamburger, only to return home the same day. The world of motorcycling opened up a whole new world of adventure to me, one I never knew existed until that first ride with Terry.

Motorcycling can take you on many adventures.

Many describe "finding their tribe" when they talk about getting started in motorcycling, and then the tribe within a tribe—other women whose passion is riding. My tribe is coed; I have as many male riding friends as I do female. But there is something sweet about meeting and building connections with other women who ride, women who do not need to have reassurances that riding is safe or who do not make me feel like an oddity when I talk about "helmet hair." Our conversations are different from those I have with many of my male friends: we don't talk as much about the mechanics of our bikes, nor do we feel a pressure to do so; we talk a lot about supporting each other, finding bikes and gear that fit, and where our best rides have been. My fellow riders and I may, and often do, disagree about politics, religion, where to live, or how dressed up to get for a night on the town, but we all agree that there is something magical about being on a motorcycle.

~ My first ride was with my mom. I had ridden on the back with her since I was pretty little, and when I was approaching my thirteenth birthday, I asked her if we could do a SaddleSore together. I researched and planned the route, and we did it on my actual birthday. I had so much fun! In a car, you are just staring at the road ahead with no connection to it. On the bike, you are a part of everything: the sensation of speed, the movement of the air around you, seeing things you might not otherwise see. I love to travel, and riding has taken us to places I'd never been before and that I doubt we'd have gone to if in a car. I'm learning to ride on the dirt now; my mom, brother, and I go out almost every weekend, and I'm getting good at it. In the state where I live, you can get a motorcycle license for the street at thirteen, and I took the MSF [Motorcycle Safety Foundation] class last year but didn't pass. I'm going to take it again this year, and I'm much more confident. My mom isn't ready for me to ride on public roads yet because other drivers are too crazy, but once I am able to, I know I'll be getting into long-distance riding. Something about it just excites me. ~

Voices of Women Riders

The sentiments expressed by fourteen-year-old Annabelle are like many I have heard from other riders with whom I have spoken, with the added delight of her youthful exuberance. Initially a bit reserved, her face began to glow with excitement when she talked about the SaddleSore, and, without her conscious awareness, her body gently swayed with remembrance as she described the feeling of being on the back with her mom. Her disappointment in not passing the MSF test the first time was quickly replaced with her growing sense of accomplishment as she described her dirt riding. The confidence in her ability to pass the next time, and the knowledge of exactly what she wanted to do in the future, was delightful to see in someone just getting started in riding. She's one of the lucky ones, with a mom who rides as both a role model and a cheerleader, and the bond between the two has clearly been strengthened as a result. Listening to her brought back vivid memories of those first moments when I first fell in love with motorcycles. I only wish I had started as young as she did; I can't imagine all of the adventures I'd have under my belt today.

One of the many common themes to emerge when speaking with other

Young women are present in significant numbers in riding classes of all kinds.

riders is movement; a felt physical sense not readily duplicated elsewhere. Motorcycling is a visceral experience, a thing of beauty when it all comes together. Gliding through curves, swaying from side to side with the motion of the bike, zipping around the bends and corners on a local racetrack, navigating dirt roads while dodging rocks and potholes: it doesn't matter where a rider is going, the journey is the event, and the journey is physical. Riders often describe cars as "cages," and when comparing a cage to a motorcycle, riders will tell you that the bike always wins. Even in a convertible, where you can feel the wind and experience your surroundings to a far greater degree, the automobile cannot duplicate the motion of tipping from edge to edge in the curves. It's a dance—smooth and effortless, graceful and elegant.

> *When I think about riding, I get a feeling, a sense of what I am about to experience; I never realized how physical my connection to riding was. My body gets as excited as my brain.*

~ *I was never a very good skier, and I found myself becoming less and less interested in putting on all the gear and hitting the slopes. When I began riding, I realized I was pretty good, and I kept working at it, getting better and better. Within a short time, I noticed that I was no longer worrying about how to operate the bike and realized that I was simply riding. Unlike my skiing days, I don't think twice about putting on motorcycling gear because now it means that I'm going for a ride. I know I'm going to have a great time; instead of dreading it, I look forward to it!~*

As with any sport, building confidence comes from building skills, and the greater the confidence in your skills, the more fun the activity becomes. Spending time, and often investing money, in learning to ride more proficiently pays off in the long run. Not only are you becoming a safer rider, you're becoming someone

> *"In a car, you're always in a compartment, and because you're used to it, you don't realize that through that car window, everything you see is just more TV. You're a passive observer, and it is all moving by you boringly in a frame. On a cycle, the frame is gone. You're completely in contact with it all. You're in the scene, not just watching it anymore, and the sense of presence is overwhelming."*
>
> —Robert M. Pirsig, *Zen and the Art of Motorcycle Maintenance: An Inquiry into Values*

A ride can be magical when you fully experience the landscape around you.

who experiences more joy in riding. Beginner riders are paying attention to the mechanics—where is the best line through a turn, how far do I countersteer to make this turn correctly, how fast should I be going in these conditions—all of the basics that a rider needs to learn. But once you've mastered the basics, the riding becomes more and more effortless, procedural memory takes over, and what was once work becomes pleasure. Groups of riders love sharing their stories of transitioning from novice to experienced and of the joy that comes from being able to hop on two wheels, start the engine, and get out for a ride. The narratives change from "I was nervous at first" to "I love the freedom, the motion, the curves, the speed"—from tales of anxiety to ones of sheer pleasure. Faces reflect joy, laughter accompanies the details of early mishaps, and heads nod during discussions of those great roads or purely magical rides when you realize that you have the entire landscape to yourself.

> ~ I found my family, my community, when I started riding my Harley. The friendships with other bikers, both men and women, the laughs we have both when riding and when stopped, the experiences we've shared; I've never had that with others before. I'm not into shopping; I'm into getting out and riding, and these friends get that! I joined a women's riding group as well, and I love the times we go out together. Sometimes, we plan a weekend camping trip, loading our gear on the bikes, riding to a beautiful place, and then spending the evening hanging out, drinking a beer, and sitting by the fire. It's been so cool to find this kind of group.~

Finding, or creating, a community to ride with often fulfills a need for connection and friendship that many may not have even known they were inclined to desire, let alone fully embrace. Social events, day rides, camping trips, competitions, or an afternoon on the track bonds riders with shared experiences and creates friendships that transcend politics, religion, and socioeconomic differences.

The better I get, the better the ride. At first, I worked on my skills to avoid accidents and to be a safe rider, but then I realized that the more my skills improved, the more I had those amazing moments—times when it all came together effortlessly. Continuing to work on my skills means more of those moments.

Even riders who prefer going off on their own frequently enjoy the camaraderie of meeting others to share a beer and a good story when the ride is over. I recently met a group of Harley riders who gather weekly to trace the identical 400-mile loop, including a stop at the same restaurant for lunch every time. Their bikes were sparkling in their polished cleanliness, and their pride in their machines was evident. Their grins spoke even louder: riding as a group was, for them, several hours of pure pleasure, and it was clear that it was something they all looked forward to during the week as an escape from the pressures and demands of their work. They were outdoors, they were sharing a beautiful ride, and they were sharing a special friendship that only other riders understood. The route they took didn't matter as much as the time they spent with each other on their bikes.

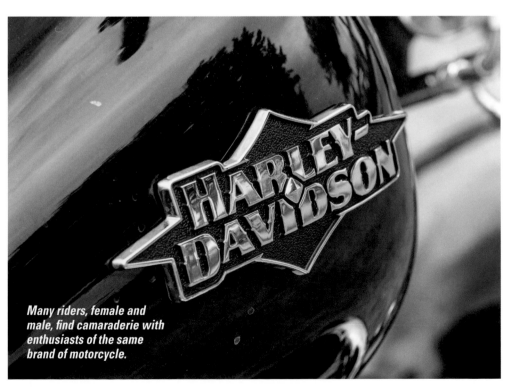

Many riders, female and male, find camaraderie with enthusiasts of the same brand of motorcycle.

~ I love riding because it drew me out of my shell and found me a family where I felt that I belonged. I first ventured into scooters at thirty-one, initially because I wanted a more fuel-efficient way to commute. But a friend encouraged me to find other scooterists to ride with, knowing that I was alone in a new town with no friends outside of work. I was extremely shy about trying to meet new people, and it was easy for me to hide. I was recently divorced, working long hours in a job that had me wading through human suffering and broken minds on a daily basis. Work was the only life I knew, and I feared it was all I'd ever have. I now have many brothers and sisters to love, lessons and merry mishaps to learn from, adventures to embark on, and memories to make and share. When I transitioned from my scooter to a motorcycle, my circle just grew larger. Riding has cost me time and money. Riding has broken my bones and broken my heart. Riding may eventually take my life as well. I still ride because it's given me a life to live, a family to love, and a place in the world. I started riding to get to work; now I ride to get to life. I ride because it makes me feel alive and full of possibility. I hope in the end, when it's all over, that I will meet my friends again and we can continue to ride and laugh and ride some more.~

Many people, especially nonriders, focus on what's dangerous and scary about riding. But in doing so, they often miss what motorcycling brings to many: a deeply felt sense of belonging and a willingness to live fully, knowing that life can be short. And, for some, what motorcycling brings may be the very thing that saves

This group of female bikers volunteered together at a road-cleanup event.

them from a lifetime of loneliness and isolation. I've dealt with the pain of losing friends to accidents, and, each time, I've reflected on my decision to get back on two wheels. When I was in my late twenties, a dear friend's husband died in a commercial plane crash. My immediate reaction was to pull those I loved close to me and essentially lock them inside a safe space. My next reaction was the

I rode the first six months with a boyfriend, and all I kept thinking was, "I want one of my own." He talked me into getting a Sportster, and I kept questioning my choice. It was hard to handle, and it never felt right. I finally realized that it was the bike he thought I should get, not the one I wanted. I traded the bike in for a Dyna Super Glide, dumped the guy, and never regretted either decision.

realization that I would merely be consigning them to a life of misery; I'd be slowly strangling their spirit. The conclusion I came to then, and continue to arrive at with every tragedy, is that life is full of risks. Mitigating those risks is important, and I believe it is the responsibility of every rider to do so. But what riding brings to my life, and clearly the lives of so many others, far outweighs those risks. I once read that since we are all going to die, we need to live a life worth dying for. It has always stuck with me: what do I want my life to stand for? Genuine connections with others and experiencing life fully are at the top of my list.

I was surprised by the number of women who were introduced to riding through a boyfriend, ultimately left the relationship, and took up riding on their own. Forever appreciating the men for opening up the world of motorcycling, they often gave no thought to losing them but would have felt tremendous regret had they given up riding. Once they began biking, they often rated finding a man who rode as a high priority. Many a woman didn't care if the man was interested in motorcycling as long as he understood that he was never going to stop her from riding. In short, no man was going to ever get between a woman and her bike. One went so far as to say that she'd never date a guy who was "too manly" to sit on the back of her bike if he didn't already ride. A surprising number of ladies actually preferred keeping motorcycling as something they shared with groups of other women, much like some women have their book clubs or tennis teams. They had no desire to bring their male partners into their riding world; if the men wanted to ride, let them find their own group.

~ *When I was in my early twenties, I really wanted to ride a motorcycle, although I'd never even touched one before. I had no friggin' idea why, but it stuck with me. Several years later, I took an MSF class and went on my first trip, 500 miles tent camping in Joshua Tree, California. I felt so profoundly connected to the world around me that I knew I'd found my passion. The more I kept riding, the more I realized how much I needed to learn, and I started reading books, following online forums, and going out with others who were better than me. To this day, every time riding is a unique day in riding: sometimes it's all wrong, and some days it just hits that sweet spot. I love the intense focus of riding; my worries fade away, and I am just in the moment.~*

For many, motorcycling touches such a raw nerve that it becomes something that the rider is unable to imagine giving up. The connection is deep and profound, and few are able to adequately put it into words. It is a visceral experience that some describe as almost spiritual. Listen to a group of motorcyclists talk, and eventually someone will share that moment when they first fell in love with the bike. Heads all around the room will nod in silent acknowledgment.

~ There's a bit of the rebellious child still in me. Riding motorcycles speaks to that part of my youth that flaunted the rules and expectations placed on me. I may be older now, but I like continuing to defy authority, although perhaps not quite as wildly as before. For me, that means riding without a helmet, my hair blowing in the wind, taking chances, and feeling free.~

In some states or countries, wearing a helmet is a matter of choice.

Having a choice of how to ride is an important theme for some bikers. While common sense and accident statistics may dictate that going without a helmet is a senseless risk, many crave the sense of freedom it offers and the feeling of

camaraderie with others who feel the same way. Some groups of motorcyclists in particular relish the culture that celebrates the Easy Rider image and rejects the confines of protective gear, seeing it as a form of interference: "Don't tell me what to do or how to do it; it's a free country, and I get to decide for myself." For others, riding a particular brand of bike and wearing gear with a certain label may convey the same rebelliousness without necessarily forgoing the desire to be safe. For these riders, the critical component is the element of choice.

The exhilaration of motorcycling can bring sheer joy.

~ I rode horses as a kid. One day, when I was seven, I was playing at the local park, and a guy rode up on a motorcycle. I was fascinated as he parked it and took off his helmet. He had shocking long white hair, leathery skin, and the bluest eyes I'd ever seen. He talked to a group of us, describing his ride across the country, and, as he did so, his eyes lit up and sparkled. I decided right then and there that when I grew up, I wanted to get a motorcycle and do whatever it was that he was doing. It's funny: my mom was terrified of me riding motorcycles but never horses, so I had to wait until I left home to get my license. I bought a cheap dirt bike and taught myself to ride out in the desert. It was so damn much fun! But even then, I had to hide it from her, or she'd freak out. Got a street bike about a year later. The first dealer I went to ignored me completely—I guess assuming that, as a woman, I wasn't going to buy anything. That ticked me off, so I went to the Suzuki dealer down the street, where the salesman was really helpful. As I rode past the other showroom on my new bike, I honked and waved at the guy who had ignored me, thinking what a jerk he had been to dismiss me simply because I'm female. My first rides were solo, not knowing other women [riders] until I met one while on a trip. We rode and camped together for a few days, and, over the years, I met more and more women who were like me. I read about Fran Crane's forty-nine-state ride in a magazine and thought it was amazing that this woman, and these riders, have the same passion that I do.~

For many, riding offers a chance to de-stress and refresh.

No matter what style of motorcycling you end up enjoying, there is something special about finding others who share your excitement. Racing, off-road, long-distance, touring the world on two wheels—it's a powerful experience to swap stories with others who understand why you do what you do. Traveling on a motorcycle is unlike traveling any other way; you are intimately connected with your environment, and, as many women have noticed, people are more inclined to approach you, creating special memories that you may miss when in a car. Meeting up with another rider, it's not uncommon to ride together for a while and perhaps spend a night or two camping, building friendships that can sometimes last a lifetime. Unlike years ago, when women riders were few and far between, today there are groups for women springing up everywhere. It's hard to go far before spotting another female out on the road, either riding solo or with others.

> ~ I initially got a bike as a cheap form of transportation, but now I use it by choice. I live far enough from work that it's a hassle to deal with traffic every day, and by riding a bike, I'm able to use the carpool lane. Parking is easier; I can always find a space, and it's usually cheaper as well. I don't really ride for recreation; I do other things on the weekends. But compared to commuting in a car, costs of maintenance are lower and I use less gas. It's an all-around win-win.~

Whether you use a motorcycle exclusively for commuting or—as a bonus—ride for pleasure in addition, there are many benefits. Especially in areas with decent year-round weather, riding offers an inexpensive alternative to a car or the bus, and many describe the ride home as a great chance to decompress from the pressures of work, arriving at the house relaxed and ready for a pleasant evening.

She laughed as she told me this story, and I knew that there was a lot of truth mixed in with the humor. Whether you need to get away from children or the mundane demands of day-to-day life, the focus needed to ride offers a welcome break. In the mental-skills seminars I conduct with motorcyclists, one of the first questions I ask is, "If I told you that you'd never ride again, what would you miss?" In every single group, someone shouts out, "The alone time in my helmet," and I see all heads nodding in agreement. Getting away from responsibilities of daily life, clearing the cobwebs after a frustrating day at the office, or letting go momentarily of having to answer to anyone else conveys a sense of freedom that can be difficult to find elsewhere. Even joining others who have no connection to your world for a few hours of riding often creates the relief needed to gain new perspectives and appreciation.

I was a single mom, and when my kids were teens, I really needed a break. Getting my license and going out riding gave me the respite I needed from the demands of parenting. I had no desire to take them with me; I wanted, and needed, the time to myself. Just a few hours away, and I was ready to go back and face my responsibilities again, but now with a smile on my face.

~ *After a bad week at work, I look forward to getting on the bike, pushing myself, and experiencing the adrenaline rush of competing. Everything that was hanging in my mind is gone. I enjoy the time away from the pressures of the rest of my life. There's a common motorcycling expression: "a bad day on a bike is always better than a good day at the office." It's definitely true for me.~*

Early female riders often learned from their fathers or their brothers and pursued their passions either alone or with groups of men. Many of these women were also mechanically inclined, needing to repair their own machines when out on rides. A lot of them are still riding today, having paved the way for those of us who follow in their footsteps. Many women are also discovering the joys of working on their own bikes, finding in themselves a passion for tinkering previously undetected.

~ *My brothers were both mechanics, and, as a young girl, I became interested as well. I bought my first motorcycle back in 1970 with earnings from my first summer job, and one of my brothers taught me how to ride it. I did all the repairs and maintenance on my bikes myself. I never saw another woman riding in those early days and didn't know there were groups for women who rode. It's been nice to see the growth of women riders over the years.~*

~ I started riding when I was six; my dad taught me. I fell in love with racing and began meeting a lot of friends at events. The more I achieve, the more I want to do better, so that's always been the challenge—to see if I can improve. I broke my ankle once, and the greatest frustration was being forced to sit out until it healed. As soon as it did, I jumped right back on the bike. When I ride to have fun, I win. The best part of riding, even more than the adrenaline of racing, is all of the friendships I've made, the bonds between all of the riders, and that we all "get" each other.~

Molly sums up what a lot of competitive riders describe: the thrill of speed, the intensity of the challenge, the desire to improve, and the community of fellow motorcyclists. There's no need to explain why she does what she does, no need to defend the risks she is taking. Everyone understands her passion for riding, her willingness to go all out, and the satisfaction of completing a difficult event.

~ My parents divorced when I was young, and I lived with my mom during the week. My dad would come to pick me up on the weekends on his bike, and it became a bonding experience for us. We'd go for rides, and I loved being on the back: the feeling of motion and the places we'd visit. When I was old enough to get my own license, I took the MSF class and got my endorsement. My dad and I still rode together, but now on two bikes. I kept asking him to go on longer and longer trips until we did a SaddleSore: 1,000 miles in twenty-four hours. I'm proud of my accomplishments, and it's been cool to share them with my dad.~

Women have achieved major accomplishments on their bikes. Here, Kate Johnston celebrates her record-setting ride.

Motorcycling can bring families together, especially when parents expose their kids to riding while they are young and encourage them to learn to ride independently as they get older. Whether long-distance, racing, or off-road, the shared experiences bond kids with their parents, creating memories that last a lifetime. Additionally, kids who learn to ride build confidence in their ability to navigate their way through problems and find solutions on their own, with their parents often their loudest cheerleaders. Falling off the bike and being encouraged to get back on teaches kids in real time—not as an abstract concept—that they can overcome obstacles. Most parents who ride are willing to let their children learn that bumps and bruises are part of living fully because it still happens even with experienced riders. Watching families riding down Forest Service roads or on challenging hills and obstacles on an off-road course and then sitting around a campfire later in the evening, sharing their adventures, or seeing the sense of accomplishment in the eyes of a young woman who has just completed her first solo long-distance ride, you know that you are witnessing something special. Doing the activity together, rather than simply watching while a child competes, forms deep connections and lasting impressions.

The bonds formed by female riders extend to off-road time, too.

~ *I didn't have a lot of money, so I was looking for a cheap vacation. My boyfriend suggested we take his bike, so I hopped on the back. I'd previously sworn that I'd never ride on my own, but when we ended up at a motorcycle rally and I attended a Women Who Ride seminar, I found myself thinking, "Hey, I can do that." Besides, I was so sore after being on his bike—it didn't fit me well, and the seat was uncomfortable—that getting my own motorcycle started to sound good. I went home, took the MSF course, and never looked back.*~

Many women fall into riding, whether solo or as pillion, never intending to get on a motorcycle until one day they do, and the love affair begins. While there are definitely those who take one ride and opt never to get on a bike again, there are many more for whom riding becomes a surprising passion and an addictive hobby. Learning to ride and meeting others who share their interest, motorcycling evolves from a fun way to spend some time into a way of life.

What some female riders once considered out of the realm of possibility or interest can suddenly become a torrid love story in the blink of an eye—or, in this case, a six-part TV series and a week of lessons. Women who have never envisioned themselves as hard-core dirt riders suddenly discover that the challenge of navigating tree roots, ditches, and deep

I watched the movie Long Way 'Round and was hooked by the off-road riding and the places they were able to go. I immediately bought a dual sport bike and took lessons. It was incredibly challenging, which I found that I loved. The people were so supportive, cheering each other on as we tackled increasingly difficult terrain. I was exhausted, beat up, and completely in love with dirt by the end of the class.

Becoming a confident rider means being able to deal with whatever the weather and the road hand you.

sand brings out an inner strength and determination to succeed that they don't find elsewhere in their lives. Learning with and riding with other women encourages them to try new skills and to become comfortable falling, getting covered in dust and mud, and picking up their bikes to keep on going. Heading out with other females also often provides a woman with a sense of safety—and comfort—in being able to say "enough" when the road becomes too hard, or conversely, enables a woman to become her friends' loudest cheerleaders when they tackle something that only moments before had completely intimidated them.

Once intimidated when confronted with simple mechanical problems at home, women riders find themselves getting down on their hands and knees to solve the same problems after they've gained skills by working on their own bikes. Wrestling a 500-pound motorcycle over logs and through deep sand makes other efforts seem simple. The realization of confidence pops up over and over when I listen to women talk about riding: "That which once terrified me no longer has a hold on me." "I feel as if I can do anything if I can ride a motorcycle." "I was shy around strangers, but now I can talk to anyone. If I don't know what to talk about, I can always start with something about the bikes."

I felt like I was having a panic attack during the entire class, but I kept gaining confidence the more I rode, and I loved that feeling; it eventually overrode the panic. As I keep gaining confidence, I keep getting more and more comfortable. I find that those feelings are transferring into my daily life: I'm less afraid to try things that once scared me.

You can quickly break down barriers when you meet another motorcyclist. In riding gear and with helmet hair, we all look the same; no one is the CEO or the hairdresser or the movie star—the labels disappear, and the titles are irrelevant. Everyone is simply a motorcyclist, and you can start conversations easily with stories of what bike you ride, where you've been, and if you know so-and-so who also rides. Talking to strangers becomes easy and fun. But confidence can also show up in even more unexpected ways.

> *~ I hated all things mechanical. I even hated putting gas in my car until I started riding. But it's weird: once I started taking care of my own bike, I found myself curious about how it worked, and soon I was in the garage, figuring out how to fix things. I discovered that I liked doing things when I was invested in outcome, and it changed how I prepared for trips and even how I ride. I still don't love filling up the tank, but that's because I hate the interruption to my riding, not because it has to do with maintenance. Although, when I think about it, filling the tank means I'm about to keep going! ~*

I had a similar experience when I first started riding my own bike. As pillion, I had no interest in maintenance or in making any of the numerous decisions that we needed to make to prepare our bike for long-distance rallies. It wasn't until I got on my own bike that the details became important. Where exactly did I want the GPS to be located? How could we plumb the lines for the auxiliary fuel cell that I needed to increase my mileage? Which tank bag was the best for holding my snacks and such? But more than noticing my increased investment in what went where on my bike, I noticed an increased interest in how it all came together. I wanted to do more of the work myself, feeling a definite difference in my pride of ownership. This was my bike and these were my problems to solve, and it was now up to me to understand how things worked. I, too, noticed the feeling of competence and confidence growing in direct proportion to my involvement, and while I still may not love all things mechanical, I do experience

Rain only adds to the fun in the dirt.

an increased sense of accomplishment that has transferred to other areas of my life. It is interwoven with all of the positives I associate with riding and is an unexpected part of what I have come to love about motorcycling.

Women motorcyclists are not just an American phenomenon: this female rider is part of a motorcycling group in Italy.

~ I absolutely love the thrill of race days on the track. I find it invigorating, challenging, and confidence-building. I started going after I had a high side get-off on a mountain road. I was riding stupid: too fast for my skill level. I decided that I needed to get smart and learn what I was doing and that if I was going to do something stupid, at least it was safer on the track. It's never been about racing; I'm probably one of the slowest ones there, but, hey, I'm a sixty-two-year-old grandmother whose twelve-year-old grandson thinks she's cool. Everything I do is about improving: I take lessons with an instructor, watch others and absorb what I see, and practice skills that easily translate back to the street. Don't get me wrong: I do love going fast, I just prefer doing it at the speedway!~

Some riders love racing, others love the camaraderie, and still others like taking what they learn on the track back to the twisty roads and tight turns that they ride at home. There is an excitement about putting on leathers, getting onto a sport bike, and seeing what you are capable of, whether you are testing yourself against other riders, the clock, or simply your own sense of accomplishment. Track days offer a chance for nonracers to come out and take a turn on the course, and many more track schools are offering women-only days in response to the growing demand.

While schools often provide bikes and rent leathers to those who don't already own them, track days typically see a wide variety of bikes coursing through the turns. Some have special "get to know your bike" days on which motorcyclists can bring out whatever they ride, including scooters, to learn how they perform at higher speeds and with cornering. It's a great chance to practice skills even when you have no interest in knowing how fast you can really go but want a chance to experience, just for a moment, the thrill that racers describe.

"If you don't try something you want to do, whatever that is, you don't have any stories to tell."
—Mary McGee, *Vintage Racing*, April 2013

~ So much of our lives are spent in separate pursuits: work, chores, even some of our other hobbies. While I could probably learn to ride my own motorcycle, I look forward to riding on the back with my partner. Being on the same bike brings us together and creates a closeness that we treasure. I like the shared space and the shared connection. I can feel him, touch him, and put my arms around him. We're so busy in life that it slows us down and helps us connect. Consequently, I have no desire to ride my own bike; this is our "us" time.~

A common theme among two-up riders is the shared experience of seeing places, meeting people, and being in the same space when everyday life so often pulls them apart. Couples share unique adventures when out on the road that can create common memories when back at home. My husband and I have countless stories of places we've been, thrilling moments of coming around corners to sights that have taken our breath away, tales of freezing rides in the middle of the night, and the shared relief of remaining upright after hitting a deer. What makes these memories even more special is that we were in all of those moments together; neither one of us is filling in the blanks, trying to explain what happened to the other. When we were on the same bike, there was a sense of closeness that added to the experience. He could reach back and touch my leg; I could massage his shoulders when he was tired. It was nice to let him be responsible for the riding and for me to take charge of the navigation, each of us having a role in whatever trip we were taking. When I switched to my own bike, the main thing that we both missed was the physical proximity.

Pillions described the pleasure they derive from assisting their driving partners, and a few even mentioned a sense of security in knowing that if something happened, particularly something bad, it would most likely happen to both of them together. This, along with having complete trust in their partners' ability after riding with them over many miles, actually decreases any sense of worry about the dangers of motorcycling. Many passengers

I never rode on anyone else's bike; I've always had my own, but my favorite riding companion is my husband. We love taking trips together and taking turns leading and planning while still sharing the same experience.

"It takes more love to share the saddle than it does to share the bed."

—Anonymous

relish the freedom to simply relax and enjoy the ride. Some enjoy taking pictures of the scenery that they have the time to study while the driver is focused on the road, while a small segment simply pull out a book and give themselves permission to escape through both the ride and the written word.

Having switched from pillion to driver of my own bike, I understand the joy of continuing to ride with my husband. Although I go on many rides without him, my best memories are with him. I love plotting routes, researching unique small towns to visit, and finding great roads to get us there. He prefers tackling the mechanical details of getting the bikes ready for the journey. We both get excited as we start packing and deciding what we will need, whether for a simple day trip or a month-long camping adventure visiting the national parks in numerous states. Having someone to bounce ideas off and listening to input about which route might be best is as much a part of the trip as the riding itself. Heading up our dirt road at the start of any ride brings a shared sense of excitement, and being on two bikes has only given us more room for gear. What is different is that I am more fully involved in every single part of the ride, and, to a much greater degree than when he was the sole driver, our conversations revolve around road conditions, weather implications, and fatigue.

Along with other couples who ride together, we are still cocreating memories. We can look back on situations that have strengthened our bond and our intimacy. We can flip through photos of places we've been and remind each other of details we may have forgotten. We spend days, and often weeks, together rather than apart. I know how he thinks and how he'll handle certain circumstances, and that brings us closer. He knows the same about me. He gets what I'm talking about when I go on about which bike to get next, and he wants to be part of that conversation. I, in turn, share his interest in which intercom to purchase for our helmets. The trivial becomes exciting when done in tandem. Rather than building these memories alone or with a friend, I'm building them with the person with whom I've chosen to spend my life, and motorcycling is fully interwoven into that process.

Competing together, whether two-up or side-by-side, creates a passion and intensity that we enjoy as we are challenged to work to solve a complex problem.

Another common refrain from couples is that adding competition to the mix has, for the most part, served to enhance their relationships. It's not unusual for one partner to be more intense than the other, but having to figure out the right balance becomes part of the process of sharing the experience. My personal stories echo these sentiments. Terry and I are forced to work through our differences "on the clock" and come to compromises quickly while making sure that we each feel heard and understood. We've learned to let go of taking care of each other and to trust our decision-making about how we ride.

I've had to learn to speak up instead of always deferring to Terry's expertise; because he's been riding so much longer than I have, I often believed that he knew what was right for me instead of trusting my own instincts. Motorcycling, compared with many other sports, levels the playing field. Unlike other athletic pursuits in which strength, size, or rules about gender might separate us, riding is something that we can share equally. Our common goals of having fun and enjoying the journey mean that we ride in a way that keeps us together, whether competing or sightseeing. The result has been far greater than expected: we have learned much more about each other and ourselves in the process, and our shared experiences, those both positive and negative, have only deepened our relationship.

~ *Riding pillion with my wife, I have total trust in her. I never really wanted to ride on my own until I met her, and when I first started, we lived in Hawaii—more rural, less traffic, no trucks, no interstates. When we moved back to the mainland, I found myself riding less and less on my own and looking forward to riding together. I like looking around and taking in the scenery, and, having my endorsement, I think I am a better pillion. We have to communicate clearly and figure out how to deal with the limited personal space we have. I think it brings us closer together when we solve those problems. It's also fun to see the reactions from others when we take off our helmets; they always assume she's a man since there are two of us. Once they get over the shock, they are full of questions and curiosity and think what we're doing is awesome.~*

Many riders, for a multitude of reasons, prefer riding pillion to commanding their own machine. For some, it's a matter of practicality, such as a lack of night vision or the cost of owning two bikes. For others, it may be fear of riding solo after an accident or simply not feeling confident on their own. But, for many, it's a clear choice: "I like the freedom to not pay attention and to let my mind wander, taking in the sights and not worrying about traffic or deer or anything else."

Listening to groups of women sharing their unique stories in different seminars I have attended, I find that there are varying opinions, differing styles, and a wide range of experiences within the room. It's easy to imagine the riders breaking into cliques like the ones many of us experienced in junior high and high school, although with different labels: the off-road riders, the Sturgis attendees, the

"I only ride on Sundays" group, those who hardly have money to afford a used bike, and those for whom a full-dress Harley barely dents the budget. I have witnessed bits of that fragmentation: certain motorcycle riders will only wave at those with the same brand of bike, some roll their eyes at other riders' cutoffs and tattoos, and others label those who will ride only German bikes as snobs; we've all heard stories. But what I see far more often is the camaraderie, the community, the desire to share, and the need to connect. The vast majority of motorcyclists understand the urge to get out in the fresh air, get away from the hassles of everyday life, spend some helmet time alone, and ride some great roads. Some of these riders may prefer to travel the world alone on their motorcycles, but when they return at the end of the day, they often want to be with others who share their interests. Within the community of women riders, there seems to be an eagerness to find those who understand your passion as well as a desire to support those just beginning their journey. No matter what reasons you may have for riding, there is room in the tent for all of us. There is no single or right way to ride; what is important is to be smart and safe, to return home ready to ride again the next day, and to enjoy the friendships that develop along the way.

Is Motorcycling for Me?

Giving yourself permission to figure out for yourself what role, if any, motorcycling plays in your life is crucial, for both your safety and your sanity. Feeling pressured to learn something that demands absolute attention and continual education may be a disaster waiting to happen if you ride only to avoid that pressure. Riding not to fall, or not to get in an accident, only increases the chances that what you fear most could actually become a reality. Motorcycling is supposed to be fun and enjoyable, a break from the demands in your life and an expression of personal freedom. If it's a burden and a chore, it's not going to be fun for you and may not be worth pursuing.

If motorcycling is for you, you'll know it!

Not everyone who is exposed to motorcycling falls in love, and many factors contribute to this. Sometimes the pressure to ride comes from someone else's desire to have you on a bike rather than from an internal interest. A partner may suddenly discover motorcycling and want you to join him or her in this new passion. It may come out of the blue or be something that he or she has talked about for years. You may have thought of it as more of a fantasy than a possible reality, knowing that it was never on your radar as a fun pursuit, and now it's suddenly staring you in the face. Or perhaps you thought, somewhere in the back of your mind, that you might want to give motorcycling a whirl at some point, but once you were on a bike, that thought dissolved into fear, discomfort, or simply something other than what you imagined. Is it OK not to like it? Or to be afraid and not want to conquer your fear? Of course it is! But how do you decide if your discomfort is temporary or permanent?

> ~ *A friend at work had always wanted to ride a motorcycle, and she talked a group of us into joining her for a weekend class. It was just far enough from home that it was easier to stay in a hotel together, splitting expenses. I had ridden on the back of my husband's bike and did not have a strong desire to ride on my own, but I thought it'd be fun to go with the group. While there were others in the class, our group bonded, sharing laughter and frustrations, cheering each other on when discouraged, and applauding when one of us mastered a skill. Ironically, I, one of the least interested in riding solo, passed the endorsement test, as did all of the others in our group except one: the woman who most wanted to ride. We all rode a bit after the class, but life began to intrude: I got pregnant, and [motorcycling] no longer fit into my plans. But what did happen is that the group of us, having bonded so closely during the class, continued our friendship, going on annual trips and sharing our lives in ways we never thought possible before. We still refer to ourselves the "Motorcycle Gang."* ~

The bonds made through biking last through time, no matter how often you see each other.

If the thought of getting on a motorcycle fills you with dread, sets off a panic attack, or just bores you to tears, take a few minutes to consider why you are even thinking about riding. I know I have no desire to crawl on my belly in a dark cave, leap off a bridge with only a rope keeping me from plunging to my death, or jump out of a perfectly functioning airplane. I don't really care if that lack of motivation is due to fear, dread, or lack of interest, but I do know that no matter how much my husband may love caves, I won't be joining him on an expedition anytime soon—or ever. If you have the same reaction when you see a motorcycle, it's perfectly fine for you to let others know, and you don't have to defend your decision. I don't need to show off my sweaty palms when talking about standing on the edge of a sheer cliff or reveal the flashes of panic coursing through my veins at the mere thought of being trapped in a small, dark space to feel perfectly comfortable about declining to take part in activities that I know I won't enjoy. It's no one's business but mine. In other cases, it's not fear but simply a lack of curiosity. For example, I have no desire to go on an ocean cruise. Do I really need to defend my choice to anyone? I have found that repeating a simple but firm "no thanks, not interested" will usually suffice to quiet any questioners.

~ *My husband and I always thought it'd be fun to ride motorcycles. About four years ago, we both went to an MSF class and got our licenses. Shortly after, we bought two bikes and enjoyed going out for day rides together. We even tried a bit of off-road riding, but neither one of us felt quite as confident on dirt, so we didn't do that as often. Two years ago, I had to have surgery unrelated to riding and take a year off from all activities to recover. When I went to get back on my bike, the one I loved before my surgery, I just didn't feel as comfortable. I didn't want to give up riding, but my confidence was gone, and I couldn't seem to get it back, although there was no real reason behind it; nothing bad had ever happened. Some friends invited us camping in the desert for a weekend, and they brought their quad with them. I decided to give it a try and discovered it was really a lot of fun. It gave me some of the feelings I had on the bike without the anxiety. We sold the bikes and bought quads, which so far has been a good decision for both of us. We still get to be together, and we're still enjoying the out-of-doors. I don't know if I'll get back on a bike again or not, but this works for us for now.~*

Sometimes an unexpected event can change your feelings about motorcycling, and it may have nothing to do with riding. What was once fun can turn into something uncomfortable or even worse: scary. If efforts to address your fears are ineffective, then it may be worthwhile to explore other options. Switching from two wheels to three, or even four, may provide the boost needed to keep you out on the road. Changes that occur with aging may make you feel safer with more wheels underneath you. A friend was diagnosed with an inner-ear problem that meant she occasionally struggled with balance, which was a concern on two wheels but not on three. Another friend had polio as an infant and uses crutches for mobility. He's never been able to ride a two-wheeled motorcycle with his leg braces, but add a sidecar, and he can outride most motorcyclists I know.

Being a female rider doesn't mean that you need to wear "girly" gear...but you can if you want!

Risk assessment is a critical element in the decision to ride. Circumstances change, and your willingness to take certain chances may change as well. Listening to your inner voice is paramount to knowing if getting on a motorcycle at this point in your life makes sense. Many who started riding at a young age take a break while raising a family, only to return to the bike when the children head off to college. Acknowledging that now may not be the time for riding does not mean that there will never be a right time in the future.

If, after taking a class and giving motorcycling a try, you find that you aren't enjoying it as much as you had hoped, it may be helpful to ask yourself why. The answers you discover may help give you some ideas about your next steps.

Do I actually like the feeling of being on a motorcycle? If you answer yes, but it's scary, then more lessons and practice may help increase your confidence. Take it slowly, ride bikes that are easy for you to manage, and only take on what you feel comfortable tackling. Find others to support you as you build your skills and avoid anyone who pressures you to progress faster than you want.

If the answer is no, then what is it you don't like? Would riding on the back or in a sidecar change anything for you? What about or riding on three or four wheels? Or, is it possible that, after giving it a whirl, you've discovered that you're simply not interested?

Do I like the culture of motorcycling and the people I've met as a result? Do I see myself as a motorcyclist? If you answer yes, then what will it take for you to become a good rider? Do you need to put in more time and practice to be safe and confident? Where can you meet others to introduce you to the type of riding that you're interested in? Would knowing more riders increase your enjoyment of riding? If so, how can you find them? Have you talked with your local dealer or checked online to see if there are groups for new riders in your area?

If your answer is no, then is there anything at all that intrigues you about motorcycling? Is someone else pressuring you to ride when it holds zero appeal for you? It's OK to say no; motorcycling is too dangerous to be doing it merely to please someone else.

I rode everywhere, all the time, without a second thought. My husband and I loved going on trips together, and I always assumed we'd keep doing that once we had kids. But then it all changed when our daughter was born. I felt responsible for her, and riding seemed scarier. If something happened to me, what would happen to her? I just can't see myself riding anymore.

My partner loves it, but I discovered that I hate it after taking the class. Are we able to navigate our differences? If your main reason for riding was because you wanted to share something with your partner, and it turns out that it isn't for you, are you both willing to be creative in resolving your differences? Is it OK with you if your partner rides to a destination while you drive or fly, spending time together off the bike once you arrive? Is it OK for your partner to go out for day rides with friends while you pursue a separate passion? Do you like riding as pillion but not on your own bike, and is that OK with your partner? Are you willing to go on occasional rides as a passenger? In other words, are you each willing to compromise to make it work for both of you?

You may prefer a different setup as you get older or if circumstances change.

Am I willing to spend time learning how to ride and build my skills? Do I take motorcycling seriously? Women who think of motorcycles as a trendy or as a fashion statement often approach riders and want to know where they can get a cool bike. But, as one rider put it, motorcycling is not the latest Coach purse, nor is it a new pair of shoes to go with a sexy outfit. It's far too dangerous to tackle if you aren't willing to put in the time for proper training and riding often. Too many new riders take the class, buy a bike, park it in the garage, and wind up putting it on Craigslist a year later. If you can't see yourself finding the time to ride, then maybe riding solo isn't for you.

Women who love riding want nothing more than to see the number of females getting on bikes increase. Nearly every female motorcyclist I know is eager to welcome new riders with open arms and plenty of support. Classes abound, groups are forming constantly, you can easily find women riders' blogs on the Internet, and the industry is working to keep up with the demand for bikes, clothing, and gear for women. If riding is in your future, you will find a home within the community of motorcyclists. If it turns out it isn't right for you, for whatever reason, everyone will still be glad that you stopped by for a visit.

Chapter 3

Getting Started

An empty parking lot is a great practice venue for riders of all types of bike.

The Basics

I was fifteen when a friend with a brand-new Honda 50 taught me how to ride. He'd given me a few spins on the back while he drove, and I wanted to see if I could handle it myself. After he quickly showed me the basics of shifting with my left foot, we found a deserted road in the neighborhood, and I took off. The tiny bike didn't have a clutch, which meant that I needed to concentrate only on the foot lever and the right hand brake, which came easily to me. Riding on quiet neighborhood streets, I never had to figure out traffic, and I discovered that I loved the feeling of movement and being in control of the bike by myself. At fifteen, not yet of legal age to operate a car, I especially loved the idea of driving a motorized vehicle. What made it even more thrilling was doing it without my parents' knowledge or permission. I wasn't able to ride very often, and soon I was old enough to get my learner's permit and take proper driving lessons in a car. Knowing that my mother and father would never approve of me on a motorcycle, I turned my full attention to automobiles. Although my experience was short-lived, I had tasted the thrill of motorcycling.

It wasn't until much later in life that I returned to motorcycle riding—and then, as a passenger. By time I was ready to learn to ride by myself, I had put in countless miles on the back of a bike, and I was keenly aware of how much there was to know that I had never understood as a teenager. This time, with far more knowledge of what was required to navigate larger bikes and complicated traffic, I wanted more instruction than "sit here, shift this, twist that," so I took a new-rider class. The first portion of the course was in a classroom, and while my experience as a passenger helped me understand what the instructor was talking about, I was surprised by how much I picked up from each class. There were several longtime riders in the room who had been advised to take the class for various reasons. Despite their initial bravado, they all also felt that they had learned helpful new information, even though they had ridden for years. When we went out onto the large, empty parking lot for real-time practice, I was a bit surprised to find that all I had learned at age fifteen quickly came back. Having driven a manual-transmission car for years helped as well, and I was able to quickly incorporate using my left hand for the clutch in addition to shifting with my left foot.

I appreciated the thoroughness of my instructors and their support in helping everyone in the class feel welcome. There were a few who struggled with basics, such as understanding the manual transmission—not only how to shift, but when. It interfered with their ability to focus on some of the other elements of the course and caused them frustration despite the teachers' encouragement. One woman concluded that she didn't enjoy riding and preferred being a passenger, not because of the mechanics but because she had taken the class to please her partner. The class helped her reach that conclusion as well as teaching her some things that would help her be a more informed riding partner.

I thoroughly enjoyed my time on the pavement. The bikes we used were small enough to help me feel confident and nimble enough to make me feel accomplished when I successfully completed each task. We started with very simple first steps, including getting on and starting the bike, using turn signals, stopping, and putting the side stand down before getting off. Once we had mastered these skills, we began drills, again beginning with simple skills and moving on to more complex. Riding in large circles and slowly tightening the radius, learning to stop while moving through corners, weaving in and out of cones, making right and left turns, and stopping suddenly were all part of our practice. We were given an on-the-bike test at the conclusion of the course, and those of us who passed with a high enough rating received certificates to take to our local licensing board for our endorsements.

Get It Right

Get the right skills from the start instead of picking up someone else's bad habits. It's much easier to learn once rather than have to unlearn lousy techniques later on.

Rider courses consist of instructional time as well as practice on the bikes.

My familiarity with riding and my experiences as a passenger were helpful during the course, and I passed the tests easily. I am glad that I decided to learn how to operate a motorcycle from an expert, in a class with other new riders, in a safe environment. I found out how much I didn't know. I learned how to ride and, more importantly, how to understand what the bike was doing and why. Not only did I become a better driver, I also became a better, more knowledgeable passenger.

Rider Education Courses

The reality is that motorcycling is a dangerous activity, as you will certainly hear from nonriding friends and family. Tell them that you are thinking of getting a motorcycle, and then sit back to hear the horror stories burst forth. Everyone knows someone who knows someone who has had an accident, and they hope that, by sharing their stories, they will discourage your desire to ride and, in doing so, keep you safe. Yes, it is dangerous; yes, there are real risks. Motorcycling demands respect and thoughtful consideration of your willingness to put yourself into an activity that can cause serious injury or death.

Rather than simply dismissing the naysayers with a "life is full of risks" brush-off, the best response is to work diligently to minimize the risks. What is one significant way for you to mitigate the danger? Take the proper initial steps to become a competent rider and then continually update and practice your skills. The smartest way to start is to get the right instruction in a professionally run training course. Statistically speaking, those who complete rider education courses are at significantly lower risk for accidents compared to riders who either were self-taught or learned from friends. Although the *Hurt Report*, issued in 1999, may be dated, the information it contains has yet to be contradicted: 92 percent of motorcycle accidents involve riders taught by family and friends.

Friends, partners, spouses, neighbors, and family members may be excellent motorcyclists, but those closest to home may not be your best teachers. A person's instructional style, breadth and depth of knowledge, and understanding of correct techniques, as well as the potential emotional complexities of working with someone close to you in learning a challenging new skill, can sometimes make the difference between loving and hating motorcycling. Every one of the most skillful and experienced riders I know recommends taking a class with an unbiased instructor who has no personal investment in your riding other than wanting you to do well. While this isn't a hard-and-fast rule, it is worth it to consider how you will best learn and from whom before starting on your journey to becoming a motorcyclist.

Even if you'll do most of your riding off-road, you still need a motorcycle license.

Assuming you decide to take a course to learn to ride, there are many options. Whether you intend to ride a scooter, a sport bike, or a full-dress Harley, or you choose three wheels over two, you need a motorcycling license. Requirements for licensure vary by state, province, and country. In some areas, there are specific, and different, licenses for two-wheeled and three-wheeled vehicles as well as for the different configurations of three-wheeled bikes. In many states, successfully passing a recognized motorcycling instructional course will enable you to obtain your motorcycle endorsement without further testing. However, in many other countries, you can earn your license only when your instructor believes that you possess the skills to be a competent and safe rider regardless of how many hours you've put in. Check with the laws in your area to make sure that any course you are considering will meet the requirements for earning your license.

Before jumping into a class, take some time to think about what you want to learn. Are you sure that you want to get your endorsement, or are you merely toying with the idea? There are numerous introductory classes, both online and in a classroom setting, that allow potential riders to get a taste of motorcycling without the pressure to take a full course, after which you can decide if it's for you. Would you prefer to be in a female-only group, removing any potential feeling of

Coed and all-female riding courses are available.

intimidation from men in the class? Due to the increase in women riders, more female-only courses are being offered. Providing a safe environment and group support, these classes can make an awkward experience fun and beneficial for many women new to motorcycles and riding. Never used a manual transmission and have no idea how they work? Some schools offer additional classes for those unfamiliar with shifting and clutches, thus removing a potential obstacle prior to the regular basic riding course.

In addition, think about what kind of riding you are most interested in. Are you primarily curious about on-road or off-road riding? Do you want to race on the track or go for casual Sunday rides on local streets? Investigating courses that focus on your specific needs may save you time and money in the long run. If you're not sure, starting with a basic course can help you develop your skills while you take time to discover your passion.

"The atmosphere of the [single-sex] class is different—they're not trying to outdo one another. For a long time, women were always passengers. [It's] nice to see them driving."

—Michelle Havranek, senior instructor and Utah Motorcycle Training's only female Rider Coach Trainer

The classes offered in your area usually depend on the demand from the public, the availability of instructors, and the type of motorcycle you are interested in. Local motorcycle dealers can be good resources and may be able to give you course recommendations based on customer feedback. Additionally, an online search for motorcycling courses will often yield results for nearby schools, although it may be worthwhile to travel outside your immediate locale to find a school that offers the specific type of instruction you seek.

Many schools teach enough for you to pass your endorsement test, but the real goal should be to become a successful, competent, safe, and happy rider. Taking a beginner class is only an introduction to riding; you will likely spend a few hours at most on a bike and ride a few miles in a controlled environment, such as a parking lot. Remember, upon completing a basic course, you have ridden only a small bike in a safe environment with no cross traffic, animals, or pedestrians, all while being watched and coached by an instructor. Although you may have your endorsement nestled snugly in your wallet, you still have taken only beginner steps on your way to becoming a skillful rider. Would you like to be on the road with a new automobile driver with a similar level of experience? Most of us would agree that it's crazy, yet we send riders out with limited experience and expect them to keep up with the demands of the street. Understanding the limitations of basic classes may help you understand the need for practice after you complete the course. As eager as you may be to get out there, remember that to be a highly skilled rider, you need to spend hours practicing on your

A helmet, a protective jacket, and gloves are among the gear you will need for a class.

own. Perhaps after you gain some confidence, you'll consider taking an advanced rider class with an emphasis on street smarts and accident avoidance.

While the following suggestions are far from an exhaustive list, I've recommended some courses that are appropriate for new riders. Most require participants to come to class with heavy-duty long pants, such as denim jeans; long-sleeved shirts or jackets; over-the-ankle sturdy boots; and full-fingered gloves

Motorcycle
instructors do
not recommend
riding without
protection for
your body.

(preferably leather). Some provide helmets; for others, you must provide your own. When you register for a course, the school should inform you of exactly what you will need for each portion of the class.

Most states offer MSF classes for new riders that include the hands-on Basic Rider I and II courses (BRC-I and BRC-II). These courses meet the minimum requirements for obtaining an endorsement and will help participants understand how to operate a bike and perform fundamental maneuvers. BRC-I consists of five hours of classroom instruction with an additional ten hours of shared riding time, usually in a large, empty parking lot. The course introduces topics such as learning to start and stop, weaving in and out of cones, making U-turns, navigating curves and corners, and sudden braking. Bikes and helmets are typically provided by the facility where you take your class. In BRC-II, you provide your own bike and ride at increased speeds, and the course content emphasizes improving the skills learned in BRC-I (www.msf-usa.org).

TEAM OREGON is a highly regarded, research-based training program started in 1984 and considered a model that others have followed in the years since. Their classes range from those for aspiring riders who have never been on a bike to advanced courses for those interested in practicing skills, such as cornering and tight turns, on a track. The intermediate course is specifically tailored to those who are self-taught or who are returning to riding after a long break but who have general familiarity with motorcycling (http://team-oregon.org).

California offers the Motorcyclist Training Course (MTC), which is required for any rider under the age of twenty-one and is highly recommended for all new riders. The classes are based on the Lee Parks Total Control method of teaching, focusing on the skills that they believe are necessary to not only ride well but also to prevent accidents. The MTC also offers the Premier Program, which provides further classroom and riding time as well as additional risk-management topics, such as emergency crash-avoidance techniques, dealing with fear, and more extensive street-riding skills. These classes provide motorcycles and helmets for all riders (www.californiamotorcyclist.com).

In addition to Oregon and California, other states also offer their own models for training new riders. Most of these classes have been designed to enhance the basic lessons and parking-lot practices of the Motorcycle Safety Foundation courses to address the needs of the new rider.

Atlanta Motorcycle Schools offer Street Smarts courses that include on- and off-road training, preparing riders for all types of conditions and circumstances. Their Adventure Sport classes are designed for beginners who want to learn to be comfortable on the street as well as when the pavement transitions to dirt or gravel (www.jkminc.com).

I love conducting the Women Who Ride seminars at the BMW Motorcycle Owners of America rallies. Once someone mentions her fear of dropping her bike, everyone chimes in with a story of her own, and soon the room is laughing, no longer embarrassed by what they all now know is a very common event.

Harley-Davidson is among the motorcycle manufacturers that offer instructional classes for riders.

"A motorcycle cannot fall over without an audience."
—Murphy's Law for Motorcycles #1

For those interested specifically in Harleys, the Harley-Davidson Rider Academy offers a variety of instructional courses. Many Harley-Davidson dealers offer a version of the MSF courses, providing appropriate H-D bikes and using their own certified coaches; riders must provide their own DOT-approved helmets. In addition, Harley-Davidson hosts "Garage Parties" exclusively for women where you can ask questions, make connections, and learn skills from other female riders in a fun, supportive environment (www.harley-davidson.com).

Some schools specialize in on-road training, taking you to the streets to learn real-time skills one on one with a qualified instructor. These programs allow you to tailor your coursework to your specific concerns and receive direct feedback on areas in which you need to improve. Ideally, your instructor will support you not only in learning the necessary skills to earn your endorsement but also in becoming a safe, competent, and confident rider. Some schools may require you to already have your license; others may help satisfy your state's requirements for licensure.

A dropped bike happens to every rider at some point.

We All Fall Down

There's a saying among many motorcyclists that either you've already fallen over or you soon will. What is meant by this expression is that it is not uncommon for a rider to drop a bike. Dropping a bike happens when you are stopped, the bike becomes unbalanced, and you simply fall over. Laying a bike down happens when you are moving, and that is not something that any rider wants to do or should expect to do.

The first time I dropped my bike, I was at a stop sign, about to turn right at a fairly busy intersection. One minute I was riding, the next I was lying on the ground with my motorcycle on its side next to me, the engine still running. Adrenaline pumping, I jumped up, completely flustered, and tried to remember what I'd been taught. First things first, turn off the bike. Luckily, my daughter was following me in her car and was able to come out and help. Remembering the second step, I put down the sidestand so when she helped me pick up the bike, we didn't accidently dump it if we leaned it too far in the other direction. I'm not sure that I could have faced another humiliation on top of what I was already feeling after my fall. After taking a few deep breaths to make sure that I was calm and ready to ride, I had to get back on, restart the engine, and continue making the turn despite the flurry of emotions in my gut and the swirl of thoughts in my head. I thought that I was a better rider, and I hadn't anticipated making what I regarded as such a stupid mistake.

Talking to my husband afterward, I realized that my mistake was a normal occurrence, and we were able to discuss what I had most likely done to cause it

One of the first times I rode my bike, I was feeling quite confident and maybe even a bit cocky as I pulled to a stop in front of my friend. Turning off the key, I hopped off, smiling and full of myself. My cockiness turned to total embarrassment as my bike fell over and I had to jump out of the way. In my rush to look cool, I had completely forgotten to put my side stand down. I never forgot to set the stand down again after that humiliation.

to happen. When coming to the stop, I had turned my head rather than keeping it straight, thus subtly moving my shoulders to the left, which had unbalanced my bike just enough for the weight to cause it to tip over. It was a good reminder of the importance of keeping my head up and my eyes forward when stopping, and a good lesson to reinforce what I had done correctly and to review what to do if I should ever have another fall: turn off the ignition, set the side stand, and take several deep breaths to calm down and think clearly. Despite honking horns or impatient stares, don't worry about the opinions or urgency of other drivers and focus on the task at hand before attempting to right the bike. These are all good points that I have been able to use on a few other occasions when I found myself unexpectedly on the ground.

Uneven parking surfaces, forgetting to keep your head forward and your eyes up when pulling into a gas station (instead of looking at the pump), not noticing a small patch of gravel where you need to put your foot when pulling into a parking space, forgetting the side stand—these are stories heard from riders both novice and expert. Become comfortable sharing your stories, laughing at yourself and the situation, and then learning from your mistakes so you don't have to repeat them. While it is common to drop your bike at least once in your riding career, it certainly isn't something you want to do regularly.

Taking It to the Street

The basic riding courses do a good job of teaching the fundamentals of operating a small motorcycle in a controlled environment. Climbing on an even slightly larger bike without the support and guidance of your instructor and pulling

Practicing on empty roads helps build your skills and confidence.

out onto a busy street is quite different, and it can be intimidating for many newbies. Some new riders think it best to join a group ride, where there is safety in numbers and others to offer their expertise. While it may sound appealing, group riding can actually be extremely dangerous, especially without a lot of experience. The complexity of watching out for others' different riding styles, speeds, and reactions to circumstances, typically in close proximity, can be a recipe for disaster for the new motorcyclist. Practicing alone and then perhaps with one other rider to gain skills and confidence before confronting traffic, pedestrians, animals, weather conditions, uneven surfaces, and low-speed maneuvers at busy gas stations will pay off in safety and enjoyment down the road. It's best to wait until you have mastered these basic skills before joining group rides.

~ I passed my course easily and, endorsement in hand, bought my first bike. Believing I possessed the required skills because I had successfully completed the class, I didn't bother practicing; I just headed out for a ride. I quickly discovered that I had a lot to learn. Right turns were much harder when facing traffic coming in both directions, and I found myself in the wrong lane a few times. The ground wasn't always smooth and level when I put my feet down to stop, and I dropped the bike more than once. With a lot of things going on at the same time, I forgot how to shift, and I stalled the bike. After a disastrous start, I swallowed my pride and went back to the parking lot to figure out how to master the skills I had been introduced to only in class. It was a very good decision, and my riding improved dramatically as a result.~

A number of highly successful women riders describe a mix of fear and excitement when they first start riding, even after taking their beginner classes. Getting back on a bike soon after the classes, the skills were fresh in their minds, and it was easier to remember what to practice. Borrowing a smaller motorcycle for solidifying your skills is a great way to get started. Each bike you get on will be slightly different, so spend a few minutes learning how the bike feels before starting it up and moving. Notice how it balances, where the weight is, and how it feels to simply hold it up. Familiarize yourself with the turn signals, the shifter, and how the brake and clutch feel.

My biggest challenge is my own confidence— my own belief in myself. Finding other women with whom I can express some of my emotions has been a big boost. They don't judge me, and it helps to know they've been through some of the same struggles. They offer advice and opinions without criticism. We support each other rather than compete against one another.

Many women I know spent hundreds of hours practicing basic maneuvers on back roads before ever venturing out onto a major highway. When planning your practices, think about things like time of day and day of week: when are the roads less congested or children in school rather than outside playing? Will the sun be in your eyes or overhead? Are you comfortable riding alone, or do you want someone with you? If you live in a busy city, is it possible to take your bike to a different part of town for your first few rides? If not, can you go out during quieter times of day? An empty parking lot is a great place to spend time simply riding around and practicing shifting, turns, and stops. Place cones in different configurations and challenge yourself to maneuver around obstacles and make U-turns. Even a few experiences will build confidence for the day you need to head out during peak traffic times.

Have a knowledgeable, supportive friend observe you. He or she can see things you can't. Are you turning your head? Are you getting the bike straightened as you stop? Are you looking where you are going? Be willing to receive feedback and learn from it. Expect to tip over. Develop the skill of laughing, picking up your bike, getting back on, and figuring out how to keep it upright.

Know when you are ready to gradually increase the complexity of riding situations as your skills improve. Are you able to use the turn signals without having to look down to find them? Are you shifting smoothly through turns? Can you consistently take off from a stop without stalling? Have you practiced quick stops using your front brake? Are you comfortable making right and left turns, ending up in the correct lane? Can you

Don't forget the side stand!

scan the environment around and far ahead of you? Decide what you are willing to do without pressure from anyone else. Equally important, make sure that your competence matches your confidence and that you really are ready. You want to be able to enjoy riding and do so safely. Riding a motorcycle is too dangerous to be doing it to meet someone else's expectations or timetables.

~ *I really didn't want people to know I was scared. I wanted to challenge myself with baby steps to build my confidence. I spent the first hundred or more miles riding alone until I felt I knew what I was doing. Even then, I felt tentative going out on the streets and dealing with traffic. But I eventually conquered my fears enough to enjoy riding, and now I love every minute I am on the bike. I still feel some fear, even today, but I no longer worry what others think.* ~

Practice, Practice, Practice

It's normal think about all the facets of riding when beginning: how to stop, how to make turns, how often to check the mirrors, shifting patterns, which brake to use, and how fast or slow to take a curve. When you consider elements such as traffic, dogs, children running into the street, cars suddenly turning left in front of you, potholes, rain-slicked paint striping, and gravel on the roadway, you don't want to be surprised when confronted by such unexpected circumstances. Once you feel comfortable in a contained environment, it's time to move on to real-life driving situations.

If you feel comfortable doing so, hit the road to practice with an experienced friend.

My MSF instructor talked a lot about situational awareness during class, emphasizing how important it is for any driver, whether in a car or on a motorcycle. I believed I was a good driver who paid attention behind the wheel, and my assessment was reasonably accurate. However, getting behind the handlebars on a busy street brought home quite clearly how attentive I needed to be. Bumps in the road that I might barely notice on four wheels became potential disasters on two. Road construction on four wheels meant slowing down or being irritated by the delay caused by a lane closure; on two wheels, I suddenly had to assess the road surface and how best to keep the bike moving through gravel without slipping or falling. Everything that was a nuisance in a car became a challenge on the bike. Two wheels demanded heightened focus; the margin for error was far smaller than in a four-wheeled enclosed vehicle. It was my job to remain engaged and focused on my riding, actively involved with my environment at all times, and doing so helped me become a more confident rider.

I call it "princess parking"—parking wherever I feel like it. I park where I know I can get my bike in and out. I think it's perfectly OK to park where you know you can control your bike; in fact, I think it's stupid to do otherwise.

"Motorcycling is not, of itself, inherently dangerous. It is, however, extremely unforgiving of inattention, ignorance, incompetence, or stupidity."

—Anonymous

Some motorcyclists never progress from the novice stage despite having ridden for years; their competencies remain limited because they don't make the effort to continue their education.

Experienced riders practice their skills all the time. Every ride is an opportunity to improve and move from novice to intermediate to advanced. Reading instructional manuals such as David Hough's *Proficient Motorcycling* (Lumina Media, 2013, 2nd ed.), watching videos, talking to other riders, taking additional courses, and, most importantly, spending time riding are invaluable in helping you progress.

Proactive Driving: ACT

While many people talk about defensive driving, I prefer the concept of proactive driving. As described by Bill Shaw in his editorial "Road Signs" in *Iron Butt Magazine*, proactive driving encompasses three main elements: awareness, control and training, or ACT:

1. Awareness

Awareness includes actively engaging with what is going on around you, anticipating situations that may arise, and planning how to implement evasive actions should they prove necessary. Key elements of awareness are scanning

the environment, looking for potential problems and thinking about how to avoid them before they occur, and understanding your reaction time while becoming comfortable braking quickly and safely. As you are driving, notice hidden alleyways or rows of parked cars where someone may pull out without looking; neighborhoods where children or dogs might suddenly dart into the road; fallen leaves that may hide potholes, rocks, or dips; or loose gravel around construction zones. Knowing how your bike handles and what it feels like in different conditions will help you understand how to react to any changes in a calm and focused manner.

Automobile drivers these days are distracted by talking on their cell phones, eating in their cars, putting on eye shadow—you name it. From my motorcycle, I have been astonished to witness drivers placing their phones on the steering wheel to text, women applying makeup in the rearview mirror, and even a man reading a magazine that he had propped up on his steering wheel while he used his knees to navigate. Especially at night, I watch for drivers who may be impaired from drugs or alcohol use with behavior such as erratic speeds, weaving in a lane, suddenly swerving, or anything else that looks or feels odd. I get away from such drivers by either moving past them or slowing down enough to let them move far ahead of me; I don't ever honk my horn or share any gesture that might provoke road rage or cause them to make a sudden move.

Be aware of the driver distractions that can pose a risk to motorcycle riders.

2. Control

Control refers to understanding and managing those elements of riding that are within your purview. You cannot control the actions of others, but you can continuously monitor your own bike and your environment and choose actions that enhance, rather than detract from, your safety. Knowing what you have control over and what you don't helps keep you engaged in riding and helps you return home safely at the end of the ride.

3. Training

Training means not only taking more classes to increase your skills but also remembering to devote your full attention to your riding every single time you get on your bike. Becoming complacent about motorcycling puts you in greater danger of having an accident, but consistently training yourself to stay focused and aware decreases that risk enormously.

Object Fixation

When your eyes fix on an object, you inevitably move toward it, as if mesmerized. Keeping your eyes moving and learning to always focus on where you are headed are critical when motorcycling. It's easy to be seduced by something in front of you—a bright light, another rider, an object in the roadway—and suddenly find

> *"Avoid problems, and you'll never be the one to overcome them."*
>
> —Richard Bach

yourself staring at it. The problem, of course, is that if you continue to stare, you and your bike will quickly collide with whatever caught your attention.

Practice looking where you want to go rather than at what you need to avoid. It's critical to commit to where you want to go, and the more you practice this skill, the more it will come naturally to you. For example, if you notice a pothole, immediately scan the roadway for where you want the bike to go. When following another rider, learn to keep that person in your peripheral vision while you watch the road ahead instead of looking at his or her taillights.

Create practice drills that keep you sharp. On lightly traveled highways, I often practice changing lanes without touching the stripes just to reinforce the skill of picking the line I want my bike to take.

Change Blindness

For ten years, I lived in a densely packed residential neighborhood where families frequently walked to the local parks or ice-cream shop, kids rode their bicycles to visit their friends, and adults stayed in shape by jogging with their dogs. In fact, I often walked into town, and I ran the streets regularly. Imagine my surprise when, one day, after carefully checking for cars and bicyclists at an intersection, I almost hit a jogger about to enter the crosswalk. I had looked, but I hadn't seen. I didn't expect someone to be there; I was looking for cars and bikes, not runners. I am sure that I looked right at her, but her presence didn't register. Change blindness refers to this kind of oversight: we can look right at something yet miss it.

Being aware of change blindness while riding a motorcycle is essential. The reality is that automobile drivers do not expect to see motorcycles. Even if you are riding right in front of a car, it can be as though the driver is looking right through you. In many cases, when a car hits a motorcycle, the car's driver simply did not see the motorcycle. In any situation involving a car and a motorcycle, the car has the definite advantage. It's your job as a rider to both anticipate such an occurrence and drive proactively to keep yourself safe.

Potholes, uneven pavement, and gravel (or a combination of all three!) are hazards that motorcyclists try to avoid.

Mental Skills: Getting Your Head into the Ride

Once the helmet goes on, you must focus on the road.

Perhaps two of the greatest challenges for many new riders, and women in particular, are self-confidence and dealing with fear. While some people may be very encouraging, others will offer horror stories and share their concerns with you, hoping to dissuade you from getting on a bike. Everyone knows someone who has been in an accident, and they have the compulsive need to tell you the gory details. Carrying the weight of their anxiety on top of any of your own can at times be overwhelming and, if not dealt with appropriately, can interfere with your ability to safely operate the motorcycle.

Once you have decided to ride and have taken classes from an expert, purchased the right gear, and picked the right bike, it's important to learn mental skills to help you become a better rider. Being in the present moment, listening to your gut instincts, and pushing yourself to build skills despite your anxieties are some of the important steps that will increase both your competence and your confidence.

When's the last time you sat down and savored a bite of chocolate, a glass of your favorite wine, or a tasty brew on a hot day? If you take a few minutes to read an interesting magazine article or book on your must-read list, are you able to focus on it fully, or do you find your mind wandering to what you need to get at the store for dinner? Women are experts at multitasking, and while this skill can be helpful when riding, it is also critical to be able to focus on the job at hand and not be distracted by other thoughts and feelings. If you practice staying in the present moment, it will help you when you get on the bike.

Choose an activity that you enjoy and take time to notice how often your mind wanders, even while you're doing something pleasurable. When you realize that your mind is going off on a tangent, gently bring it back to what you were doing. Taste the chocolate, feel the warmth of the bath water, look around at the scenery; it's important to focus your attention, and you may have to do it again and again and again. The more you practice this skill, the more you will find it available to you when riding. In the same way that you train your body to hold the throttle or your foot to shift smoothly, you are training your brain to return to the road, ignoring any attempts to hijack your attention.

Just as we physically go where we look, we also mentally go where we look. If you are constantly worrying about falling, you will begin to ride to not fall rather than riding to stay upright and have fun. Random thoughts, such as crashing, falling, and getting a flat tire, are actually common among riders. The difference between those who ride confidently and those who ride with fear is that the confident rider will either simply let the thought pass without paying it heed or will use a worrisome thought as an opportunity to mentally practice: What would I do if x, y, or z happened? When faced with a "what if," mental rehearsal is far more helpful than worry. Increasing your situational awareness, knowing who and what is around you as you ride, and having an escape route in mind increase your ability to stay in control should a problem arise. It's OK to have some fear. A small bit of fear, in the form of respect for the challenges of riding, may actually help remind you to pay attention. It's only when the fear consumes your attention that it can turn into a problem.

> ~ *When I was eighteen, I was at a party with a bunch of friends when one of the guys pressured me into getting on his bike behind him and riding it across a field. Not knowing better and wanting to look cool, I hopped on. He started going faster and faster, and I was yelling at him to slow down. He was laughing up until the moment we crashed the bike. I wasn't hurt, but I swore to myself I'd never get on a bike again for the rest of my life. When I got older and saw girlfriends out riding, I began to think that I might want to give it a try, but I kept having "I can't ride" thoughts. I had to figure out how to quiet that negativity so I could get on a bike and feel confident.~*

Avoidance can be a good thing when we're talking about hazards on the road or toxic people. However, it can be negative when it applies to finding reasons to avoid uncomfortable situations. When I was first riding on my own, I found myself coming up with brilliant excuses for stopping on side streets instead of in parking lots. Who was I kidding? I was afraid of the parking lot: the tight turns into a space, cars all around, slanting surfaces, and trying to figure out where to go. The more I avoided parking lots, the scarier they became. What I realized was that the thing I was afraid of was the exact thing that I needed to practice. Addressing my anxieties, I started turning into lot after lot, slowly at first, until they no longer intimidated me. I did not want to limit my riding by my fears; I wanted the freedom to ride wherever I chose to go and my skills would take me. Conquering my parking-lot phobia increased my willingness to tackle other challenges, and every successful step forward further built my confidence.

But I also know when to listen to my gut and to voice my concerns when my anxieties are rooted in a genuine fear. When I was a new rider, a friend continually urged me to go on rides with her. She had been riding for a long time. She had taken advanced classes and felt comfortable in a wide variety of situations. I had ridden pillion long enough to know that I wasn't ready for some of the roads she wanted us to take; I knew my strengths and my limitations. Although my brain wanted to go with her, my gut was telling me that I needed more practice on simpler roads. I chose to listen to my gut despite her pleadings and instead spent more time mastering my skills. It was hard to say no, but when I was finally ready to say yes, I felt confident and ready for wherever we might go.

Fueling up can be an intimidating task until you've done it a few times.

My gut instinct is different from my chattering brain voice: my gut is like a warning that something is just "off," while my brain chatter is the "you can't do this, it's too hard, it's too scary, what if you fall?" voice that isn't telling me anything useful. When that voice becomes too loud, I simply invite it to sit on the pillion seat and yammer away; I can't really hear it with my helmet on, and I don't need to pay it much attention. The more I focus on the road ahead and what I am doing, the more that chattering voice fades into the myriad of sounds and noises in the background. The voice from my gut, however, kicks me in the stomach until I am forced to pay attention, and it's one I hold in deep respect; it's kept me out of some potentially dangerous situations.

I've noticed that the words I use impact my riding. If I find myself describing something as difficult, it often becomes hard. If I use negative language, my emotions focus on the negative aspects of the experience. If, instead, I use action

language that focuses on what I need to be doing, my brain will follow. For example, after I dropped my bike at a gas station, I realized that I had been turning my head to look at the pump as I approached, thus unknowingly turning the handlebars ever so slightly—just enough to unbalance the motorcycle. The next time I needed gas, I repeated "head up, eyes forward" over and over in my mind until my bike was properly aligned and the side stand was down. Only then did I look over at the pump. Had I told myself "don't look at the pump," my brain would have focused on the word *pump*, and I would have found myself on the ground again. Pay attention to what you tell yourself and remember: we go where we look, even in our minds.

Very often, early experiences leave vivid impressions, and the more we tell a story, the more we reinforce it. With constant repetition, it becomes easy to give tales of accidents, near misses, or lousy learning experiences the power of truth. The words we use can keep us stuck and prevent us from moving forward to try things we really want to try. Retelling the narrative without the negative emotions and focusing instead on what you learned is one way to change your perspective of an event.

Imagine if the rider had described the foregoing scenario like this:

~ *When I was eighteen, I got on the back of a guy's bike. We went across a field, too fast for my comfort. We dumped the bike, and I walked away OK. I learned from that experience to listen to my gut instead of trying to impress others. I can now say no when someone is pressuring me to do something I'm not comfortable with.*~

Does this narrative reinforce her fear or her trust in her gut instinct? Which do you think would be more helpful for someone who wants to get on a bike again?

In addition to practicing these mental skills, it's important to practice how to deal with other

"Argue for your limitations and sure enough, they're yours."

—Richard Bach

people's fears about motorcycling. Letting their horror stories or anxieties get into your head can affect your focus and, potentially, your riding. It's enough to have your own brain chattering; you don't need to add a whole chorus of nay-sayers. So how do you handle it when someone feels compelled to share his or her version of "I knew someone who (fill in the blank with something terrible)?"

I have several approaches, and it's important for you to find what works for you. It's unproductive to offer explanations to those who can't, or won't, be open to changing their perceptions. Recognizing who these folks are can save you a lot of time and breath because their agenda is to change your actions, not theirs. A simple but persistent "thanks for your concern," along with changing the subject, may suffice. But for those whose opinions and concerns matter to you, the best you can do may be to share your passion for riding, your efforts to continually improve your skills, and your acknowledgment that something bad may happen and you are willing to accept that risk. Allowing someone to be scared while asking him or her to refrain from sharing horror stories is a fair request on both sides. If that doesn't work, I've sometimes volunteered stories of my own: I still fly even though my friend lost her husband in a commercial plane crash, and I did not quit driving after being rear-ended in a car accident. I know someone who was driving under an overpass just as an earthquake hit and was crushed (true story). I even share that some of my dearest motorcycling friends have died—a few on the bike, and just as many from illnesses. We don't get out of here alive, and my choice is to live fully in the time I do have. Other people are free to make choices for themselves, but not for me.

Instead of an automobile driver telling someone who rides a motorcycle how dangerous it is, ask the driver if he or she is willing to look twice before switching lanes, making turns, or pulling out of a driveway. Remind the driver to stay on the correct side of the road, especially on corners, and not to follow too closely. Encourage the person to keep his or her eyes on the road and to definitely put down the cell phone and ignore incoming texts. For those of us on motorcycles, automobile drivers' decisions and actions can truly be the difference between life or death.

Chapter 4

Improving Your Skills

Breathtaking sights and challenging roads are part of the experience.

My husband and I were training for the Iron Butt Rally, an eleven-day competitive long-distance ride. This was the first time we'd be riding it on separate bikes, and it was important for us to take the time to learn to work together in a new way. My pre-ride job was to plan our route, incorporating a wide variety of conditions so we would be prepared for whatever we might face during the event. We had to go for long rides day after day, and one of my favorites was a 600-mile day in Northern California.

I wanted to create a ride that combined several elements: lovely scenery, unusual locales, and interesting road challenges. After mapping out a route that seemed to meet my criteria, we loaded the waypoints into our GPS units and packed the bikes for the trip. We left from a friend's house at 8:00 on a weekday morning, heading in the opposite direction of commuters.

The day was beautiful—sunny but not too hot—and the first few blocks took us through rolling hills and horse pastures. Entering civilization and the hustle of morning traffic, we were able to quickly pass through a small town and turn onto the road that would take us over the mountains to the beaches near Santa Cruz. Climbing the gentle hillside, we wound through tree-lined streets, past houses tucked behind old ivy-covered rock walls. The road slowly became steeper and the turns more interesting until we reached the pass and began our descent. It was a relaxing start to a promising day, and I could smell the salty air long before I caught my first glimpse of the ocean.

Arriving in the seaside town during the tail end of the morning commute, we stopped briefly for gas before turning back toward the mountains. Had this been a leisurely ride, we would have detoured to the boardwalk for coffee and a snack, but we needed to stay focused and keep an eye on the clock. When we left the city, we headed into the mountains once again, this time through quaint small towns before turning onto a side road and into a state park. The trees quickly enveloped us on the narrowing road, and the tight twists and turns demanded my concentration. I loved the challenge, and I loved breathing in the mountain air and being surrounded by trees everywhere I turned. Emerging back into the sunshine several miles later, we returned to the main road and traversed the hills until, once again, it was time to descend into the noise and bustle of the city.

Accelerating to freeway speeds always gives me a rush; I like going fast. All too quickly, however, the freeway ended, and we were in city traffic, driving through streets lined with two-story rowhouses, each unique in its styling and décor. I love San Francisco, and today was no exception. Our next stop required us to take a photograph of the Golden Gate Bridge from the base on the south side. The view was one I'd never seen, and we stood for a few minutes to enjoy the fresh breeze and magnificence of the structure before it was time to move on and cross the bridge we had just been admiring. The height of the bike gives me views I can't get in a car, and I took in the sailboats in the distance, the pedestrians walking hand in hand along the railings, and the gulls flying overhead.

A group tackles Iron Mountain Road in the Black Hills of South Dakota, near Mount Rushmore.

Back on the interstate, we headed north toward our last stop for the day, a small town 26 miles inland along a lazy, winding road that paralleled a river for much of our journey. The hillsides were golden in the early summer sun and blanketed with trees, providing brief moments of welcome shade in the afternoon heat. The riding was spectacular, a delightful mix of sweeping curves and gradual climbs and descents. Knowing we would be returning the same way only added to our pleasure.

The final portion of our ride was once again on the interstate; it was cool and quick as the sun set and night surrounded us. The lights of the city welcomed us. As we pulled back into the driveway of our friend's home, I smiled with satisfaction: our training ride had been a complete success, and I was definitely ready for a good night's sleep.

Our training ride was a typical day trip for me as a long-distance rider. Continually discovering beautiful new roads and stunning scenery constantly reminds me how lucky I am to be on a motorcycle to soak it all in. But what lies behind the beauty is the challenge of tackling a variety of situations. The mileage I cover provides ample opportunity for me to repeatedly test my skills and reactions. Although it is not unusual to find challenging road conditions on a longer ride, I might also encounter them on a fairly routine ride. Going back through my 600-mile day, I'd like to share a behind-the-scenes look at what was going on both on the bike and in my head. How prepared would you be to react to some of the same situations?

The ocean air and the sweeping panoramas draw bikers to San Francisco.

Pulling out of the garage where our friends had graciously let us park our bikes, I had to immediately tackle their driveway. The house sits below the roadway level atop a ridgeline, and the drive slopes in multiple directions, including a small, steep hill to the street. I needed to wait for my husband while the garage door finished closing, and it took my full attention to remain balanced on the uneven surface. With my head and eyes up and looking forward, I made sure that my bike was straight.

When we were ready to go, I headed to the top of the drive to make a right turn onto the steeply downward-sloping street, making sure no one was coming from either direction. A quarter mile later, there was another right turn, this time with rough, uneven pavement and a downward cambered incline that followed the curve of my turn. A few yards farther, the road divided into two narrower lanes with a treed median to my left. The stop at the bottom of the hill was littered with bits of gravel. Barely a mile from the house, I'd already had to make numerous decisions about turns, sloping roadways, where to stop, and uneven surfaces and gravel.

Signaling for a left turn, I watched for cars exceeding the 45-mph speed limit and loose dogs before pulling out. Taking neighborhood roads, I soon arrived in a busier section of town where there were a series of traffic signals and left-turn lanes, causing confusion about where we needed to be. Adding to the chaos was a railroad crossing.

Once free from the congestion of the town, we headed out to the coast on a two-lane road, taking the scenic back way rather than the state highway. There was much less traffic and far fewer tourists than on a Saturday or Sunday; however, it was still a workday for most people, and, as we arrived in the large coastal town, we were in the midst of the late morning commute. Drivers who use these roadways daily know their ins and outs, but I was not a local. I needed to be mindful of cars, bicyclists, pedestrians, and school zones while simultaneously listening to the directions my GPS was giving me.

I had started the ride with only half a tank of gas, and I saw that it was time to fill up. I alerted my husband with our Bluetooth Sena device, and we both began

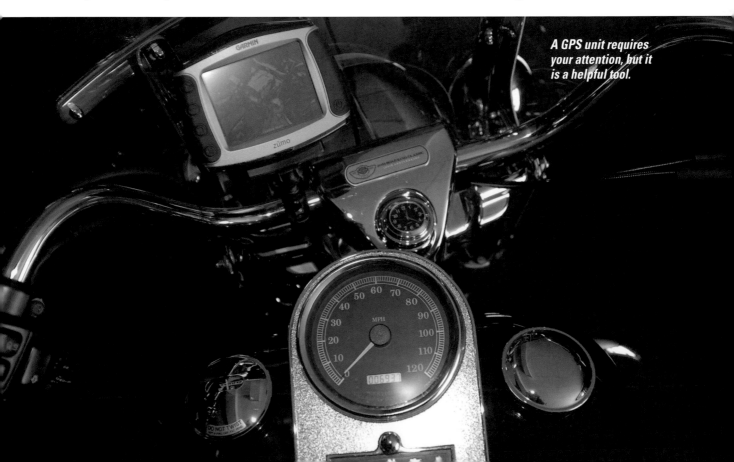

A GPS unit requires your attention, but it is a helpful tool.

A hands-free system allows safe phone calls as well as rider-to-rider communication.

looking for a station, preferably on the side of the highway that we were riding on. Our habit is for me to choose a pump and for him to pull up next to me once my side stand is down. We then share the pump and pay together. While I am now comfortable using either side to refill, my husband, only partially joking, suggested when I was first learning that I keep the pump on the right side of my bike. That way, if I dropped the bike, it wouldn't hit the pump, and it would cause less damage both to me and to the gas station.

Tanks full, we pulled back into traffic and returned inland, heading to a state park in the nearby mountains. The road was busy, and we passed through several small towns before encountering a twisty road with homes tucked into the trees as we turned toward the park. Keeping my eyes focused on the line of the curves, I used my peripheral vision to constantly watch for unusual movements or any indications that someone was stopping suddenly or pulling out of one of the hidden driveways.

The road we took through the park was even more demanding, with tighter hairpin turns and single-lane width at times. I had to make sure that I was 100-percent focused on the road and staying on my side of it. Meeting with a few cars required even more attention, and I could not allow myself to look at them or where they were going. Adding to the challenge was a phenomenon referred to as "picket fencing," which refers to riding in densely treed areas with the sun filtering through intermittently; this creates a constant flickering of light and dark that can be extremely distracting.

Neglected Roadways

Most states have limited funds for highway maintenance, and, as I travel, I see the results of years of neglect: fractures in the pavement, uneven patchwork repairs, and miles of tar snakes (tar that has been used to fill in cracks in lieu of digging up and replacing roadways). Tar snakes can heat up in warm weather and become slick, causing a scary moment as the bike tire slides out slightly, particularly if contacted on a curve at speed. They can be slippery when wet or simply bumpy if newly poured. Interstates frequented by eighteen-wheelers can surprise a rider with unexpected retread tire bits, or "gators," strewn across the lane. Hitting one could be disastrous if the steel wires inside puncture a bike's tire. Keeping the tires out of long grooves and dodging potholes or gators requires me to focus on where I want the bike to go, and watching cars or bikes ahead of me helps me anticipate bumps or other problems up ahead. Keeping enough space between my bike and trucks or large cars that block my view gives me time to react.

On the other side of the mountain, it was time for a bit of interstate and city traffic, which was a welcome break from the intensity of the twisty roads. I'd planned a quick stop alongside the bay to catch a glimpse of the bridge we'd be crossing shortly, and the road in and out of the parking area was uniquely challenging. Coming down a steep hill, I had to make a sharp, angled left turn into a narrow driveway that essentially turned back on itself while I watched for oncoming traffic and for cars that might be pulling up the drive to exit. After our brief stop, I had to make a U-turn in the parking lot to exit, navigate the return out of the steep drive, and then make a sharp right turn onto an equally steep hill.

Finally, we were on open highway for miles and miles—until road construction on the interstate caused lane closures. Cars responded with sudden moves, abrupt stops, and quick lane switches with no signaling. I focused on keeping my escape route in mind, watching for sideways lurching or hesitant moves, and assumed at all times that someone would cut me off. When the traffic began flowing again, I remained

Unexpected road construction can wreak havoc on even the most carefully planned trips.

Dealing with Deer

I learned firsthand about the erratic behavior of deer when I was still riding pillion. On a quiet back road in the mountains of Utah, we came upon a buck standing in the opposite lane, staring at us and not moving. We were already going at a slow pace due to the time of day, and we slowed even more as quickly as we could. When we were almost parallel to the deer, he suddenly leapt in front of the bike, and we hit him full on. Due to our low speed and the weight of the bike, we stayed upright while he tumbled onto the roadway, rolled over, jumped up, and ran off. Shaken but unharmed, we pulled into a safe spot to check for damage to the motorcycle before we kept riding. That minor collision, while not causing us any injury, required more than $4,500 in repairs to the bike. I have no desire to meet a deer up close again.

vigilant for a frustrated driver who was relieved to finally be picking up some speed to whip around another car and end up in my lane.

Our final stop for the day was a small town 26 miles off the interstate. We took a quiet, twisty country road and saw only a few cars as we rode. After visiting the town, we headed back on the same quiet road, but it was now after 6:00 p.m., and the sun had come down in the sky. Riding directly west, it was often shining straight into my eyes. As the road twisted and the sun went in and out of the branches, I was alternately blinded and then thrown into shadows. To make it more interesting, I saw several deer alongside the pavement. I rode slowly, constantly scanning for this unpredictable animal, knowing that if one leapt out, I would not swerve to avoid it but would brake as carefully as I could, hoping to avoid a collision.

Safely back on the interstate, it was time to head home, a distance of approximately 200 miles. The remaining portion of the ride was on major highways, which were easier to navigate but continued to demand my full attention. As the day went on, I monitored myself for fatigue, knowing that my focus might wane if I were tired. It can be easy to become hypnotized by lights and to forget to scan the roadway for obstacles in the dark, especially when tired.

Arriving back at our friend's home, I once again had to attend to the steep hills and sloping driveway—adding in the risk of animals darting across the rural road—and pull into the garage, remembering to put down the side stand after the long day. Tired and elated, I stripped off my gear and headed in for a well-deserved glass of wine, a warm shower, and a cozy bed.

Condition Considerations

Most riders will plan to go out on pleasant days, avoiding rain, wind, snow, and excessively hot or cold temperatures. After all, who wants to be miserable? However, the best-laid plans are often disrupted when sudden changes occur during a trip. Some riders live in areas where weather is a variable that they must factor into any trip. Extreme heat and humidity are common in the southern United States; wind blows furiously at times in the deserts, plains, and mountains; and rain is common in the Northwest. If you go out only on days with nice weather, you may not get out

If you ride often enough, you will inevitably encounter bad weather.

Rain-slicked roads are a given in the Pacific Northwest.

much! Learning how to manage your motorcycle in all conditions will help you be a safer overall rider even if you choose to ride only on the best of days.

One of the first considerations for any change of weather is to slow down and take time to understand how your bike handles in whatever condition confronts you. Reducing your speed will give you a chance to learn about you and your bike as well as time to react to what is happening around you.

Wind can come at you from the side, the front, or behind. It can be constant or erratic, whipping around in sudden bursts. Every bike will handle the wind differently, depending on its weight and how the weight is distributed, fairings or lack thereof, and windscreen. Being mentally and physically prepared for what you may experience will help you keep your bike on the road. Depending on the

Training for Long Distances

My husband and I have trained for long rides just as marathon runners train for their events. Marathoners don't start their running careers by entering a full race; rather, they build endurance over time and learn their bodies' cues for fatigue and injury. They train by slowly adding time and distance until they are able to tackle the 26.2 miles with a reasonable chance of success. Good long-distance riders are the same: we build mileage and endurance and learn the cues that tell us it's time to get off the road. If either my husband or I notice any changes in our ability to stay on task, we pull off and find a place to rest.

Expect the Unexpected

Being prepared to ride in any conditions will help you stay safe when the unexpected occurs. Wind, rain, heat, and cold can challenge you both mentally and physically. Having the right gear, the right training, and the right attitude will help keep you safe when the weather suddenly changes and you are forced to deal with whatever Mother Nature can throw your way.

direction it is blowing, the wind may suddenly stop when you are passing semi trucks, hills, or large structures, but it can then hit you hard or suck you in after you drive by or if you are traveling too closely. Unpredictable wind will whip you around, lurching you from side to side. Watch for wind socks on bridges, the reactions of vehicles in front of you, or debris blowing across the roadway for indications about what you might encounter. If you live in an area where you will be routinely encountering difficult conditions, you may want to take a few lessons from an experienced rider to build your skills and confidence.

I once rode 100 miles across the desert in a steady 45-mph wind with gusts up to 65 mph. Finally, I arrived at my destination, a national park visitors' center, to find the rangers surrounding a rider and his motorcycle. He was upright, but his bike was on the ground. He had parked it with the side stand into the wind, and one of the gusts had blown it over and into the ranger's truck. Putting the side stand on the leeward, or downwind, side can help keep the bike upright as the wind blows against it. Other riders choose to point the front of the bike into the wind, where less of the bike is exposed to the blowing gusts. In addition, making sure the bike is in first gear and engaged when parking acts as a brake should the wind, or anything else, move the motorcycle even slightly forward.

I live in the Pacific Northwest, and rain is a given in our area: drizzles, showers, and river-overflowing rains. I have ridden in all extremes—not always intentionally or happily, but often due to necessity. If possible, I will sit out the downpours and tolerate the showers. Slowing down, watching for slick surfaces, giving more space between my bike and cars, and wearing waterproof gear are essential for turning a potentially horrible ride into one that is merely miserable. Early rides in drizzle and thousands of miles as pillion helped me understand how

Overconfidence

Overconfidence is one of the accident predictors for those who have been riding for more than a year. Taking advanced courses is a great way to remind yourself what you need to keep doing to be safe and to increase your skills to help you face any challenges you may find out on the road.

the bike would handle in wet weather, and talking to other riders with a lot of experience taught me what to expect and how to react.

Extremes of heat and humidity can exhaust the best riders if they don't dress appropriately or hydrate sufficiently. Consuming water regularly will help diminish the intensity of the heat, and covering up will keep the wind from evaporating moisture off you and the sun from damaging your skin. While it may seem as if wearing fewer articles of clothing will help keep you cool, it often has the opposite effect as temperatures increase.

There are a few events in winter locales for bikes equipped with studded tires, but, as a rule, motorcycles aren't meant to be operated in the snow. It's best to check forecasts to avoid being caught in a sudden storm. However, light rain can unexpectedly turn into light snow, which can become a storm without warning. I've been caught twice in such circumstances; in both cases, the only option was to keep moving to stay warm (my heated gear worked when the bike was running;

Small-group instruction sometimes takes place on the road.

therefore, stopping meant freezing) and get to a safe place to stop. Late at night, on a long stretch of highway with no homes, no businesses, and few cars meant slowing down to a crawl, turning on my emergency flashers, and hugging the side of the road, away from tire tracks that might have iced over. Keeping my speed down meant I could stop without using my brakes, and I focused on where I wanted the bike to go. While I don't recommend this as part of your training, knowing what to do helped me stay safe until I could find a hotel with a warm shower and a cozy bed to wait out the storm.

Back to School

The greatest number of accidents involving motorcyclists takes place in the riders' first year after learning to ride. This makes sense because the new riders have yet to master the skills they have learned. What's interesting is that the next highest category of risk is riders who have approximately two years of experience. Why? Such a rider has conquered the basics and is confident, and it's easy for the rider to become complacent, even cocky, and forget to practice the safe riding techniques that have allowed him or her to go without incident thus far. Once you've ridden between a few hundred and a few thousand miles, it's wise to return to school.

Many experienced riders take classes regularly, always wanting to keep their skills fresh and remain accident-free.

Advanced rider courses, whether for street, dirt, or track, will improve your riding in any environment and give you the opportunity to practice in more controlled settings. Track classes will help you with turns even if you never plan to set foot on a track again. Dirt classes will improve your confidence on uneven surfaces or in those moments when you are suddenly confronted with a gravelly road. Many advanced classes include a street-school component in which the instructor rides with you on his or her own bike and the two of you are linked by communication devices in your helmets. The instructor can offer real-time instruction and feedback. Some classes also include trips and tours, with small-group instruction as you confront new situations.

Ask your motorcycle dealer, talk with friends, and conduct online searches to find the best schools for your specific needs. A program that works for someone

Recommended Resources

While far from an exhaustive list, the following are books and videos that I recommend for your personal library. These are produced by well-respected riders and offer tips, techniques, and safety measures that you can practice and improve on your own.

David Hough, an American Motorcycling Hall of Fame member honored for his relentless passion for increasing motorcycle-safety awareness, began writing a regular column for what is now *Motorcycle Consumer News* in 1984, in addition to articles in *Sound Rider* and *BMW Owners News*. His books, *Proficient Motorcycling: The Ultimate Guide to Riding Well*, *More Proficient Motorcycling: Mastering the Ride*, *Street Rider's Guide: Street Strategies for Motorcyclists*, and *Street Strategies: A Survival Guide for Motorcyclists*, gather the valuable information contained in his columns into useful and easy-to-read manuals that every rider should have in his or her library. For those interested in sidecars, his book *Driving a Sidecar Outfit* is a great resource.

Lee Parks raced for more than twenty-five years and was the editor and test rider for *Motorcycle Consumer News*. His Total Control Advanced Riding Clinics are designed to bridge the gap between beginning rider classes and track schools, and his curriculum has been adapted for California's beginning and advanced motorcycle courses. His book, *Total Performance Street Riding Techniques*, was updated in 2015 and is based on the training techniques taught at his clinics.

Jerry "Motorman" Pallindino created the Ride Like a Pro motorcycle courses and videos after completing the Florida Highway Patrol's training program and realizing that the techniques he had learned were of tremendous value, especially for riding at low speeds. His courses cover the same materials that make motorcycle police some of the most agile riders around.

Keith Code, a former motorcycle racer and the founder of the California Superbike School has been called "the best known and most successful on-track instructor in the world today" by *Rider* magazine. He's published books for those interested in the track and MotoGP, including *A Twist of the Wrist: The Motorcycle Roadracer's Handbook, A Twist of the Wrist, Volume 2: The Basics of High-Performance Motorcycle Riding*, and *Performance Riding Techniques: The MotoGP Manual of Track Riding Skills* (co-written with Andy Ibbott).

Nick Ienatsch has spent years teaching sport riding in addition to writing for various motorcycling magazines and finding time to race. His book, *Sport Riding Techniques: How to Develop Real World Skills for Speed, Safety, and Confidence on the Street and Track*, is geared toward both riders looking to learn proper techniques and those wishing to take their skills to the next level.

In addition to courses, books, and videos for motorcyclists of all ages, a series of podcasts, available for free on iTunes, is available for older riders: "Dr. Ray's Seasoned Rider eCourse," presented by the Motorcycle Safety Foundation. This series encourages riders to remain on the road while addressing declining reaction times and changes in physical ability and strength. Simply being reminded of the skills needed to be safe as we age may come in handy down the road.

else may not be the best fit for you, but it can be helpful to hear what others have to say before committing to a course.

...and Beyond

One of the most vivid images I have is of a YouTube video of a motorcyclist enjoying a twisty road right up until the moment he missed a tight turn and went straight over an embankment and down into the trees and dirt. If seeing that wasn't shocking enough, a second rider who had been following the first rider appeared on the screen. It was soon obvious that he had been watching the first bike instead of the line of the turn, and it was only a last-minute swerve that kept him from going over the same embankment. What happened? Object fixation. The memory of this video sticks in my mind, reminding me to keep my eyes where I want my bike to go.

The more I ride, however, the more I make sense of the written word as well as the visual. I understand how the bike feels and handles, and I can relate to the comments and instructions in books such as *Proficient Motorcycling*. Reading allows me to close my eyes and think about what the writer is describing, and I can mentally practice what I am learning. Further, videos and instructional manuals can refresh skills I practiced in my classes but may have not yet encountered on the road. Reviewing forgotten maneuvers helps me mentally prepare for them should they arise as I ride. Also, seeing the mistakes of other riders as well as the correct ways to ride have been useful to me in reinforcing good techniques. Take advantage of the many resources available to teach you advanced skills or refresh those you've already learned.

Keep an eye out for "gators," or tire debris, especially on interstate highways.

Extra Credit: Vocabulary

Along with the skill set I've developed while riding on two wheels instead of four, I've also increased my vocabulary. Specific groups of motorcyclists, such as Harley-Davidson riders, sport tourers, off-road enthusiasts, or long-distance devotees, develop within their culture their own unique slang, but there are universal terms for all riders, too. Becoming familiar with a few words and phrases may not only help you understand conversations with other riders, but in some cases it may help you avoid danger. The following paragraphs explain a few terms worth learning.

You're riding along the interstate, and suddenly you see a large black strip of something up ahead. Most likely it's a *gator*, part of a steel-belted tire that has come off a semi truck. These are incredibly hazardous because the steel can puncture your tires in an instant; a gator can also cause significant injury if it hits your body.

An unexpected rough patch can take a rider by surprise.

When you see one gator, expect to see more, and you must avoid them. When driving in an area heavily traveled by truckers, keep your eyes open not only for debris but also for any signs, such as smoke coming from a tire, which indicates that it may blow.

It's a beautiful, hot day, and you're enjoying a lovely ride on a two-lane twisty road when suddenly you feel your bike slip a bit in the turn. You notice the signs of previous road repairs: tar used to fill in cracks in the otherwise unremarkable asphalt. You've never noticed them before, but you've also never ridden on this road in this kind of heat when the *tar snakes* tend to show their true nature. When the tar melts just enough to become slippery, your bike can briefly slide as you ride through it. Being aware of the effect that heat has on tar can help you prepare for riding over tar snakes.

It's late in the afternoon, and you're riding up the quiet country roadway to visit a girlfriend for an evening of good food and good company, when suddenly a deer—known to bikers as a *forest rat*—leaps out from behind a tree on your right and bounds across the road in front of you before disappearing somewhere in the bushes on your left. It happens so quickly you don't even react; you catch your breath and continue up to your friend's driveway, grateful to be stopping for a while to process what just happened. This actually happened to me—the deer jumped out between my husband, who was just ahead on his bike, and me. Luckily, her two fawns weren't following her that day, and it became a

"The Wave"

When I first started riding, I noticed a lot of motorcyclists putting two fingers of their left hand out and down toward the road when they passed us. I quickly learned that this was "the wave," a common greeting among riders. I also soon learned that there are a wide variety of opinions on when, how, and to whom one should or should not wave. Apparently, some riders have very strong feelings about this friendly gesture. My solution is simple: if you are in a place where it is safe to do so, and you're so inclined, then wave. If you are in a situation in which a simple greeting would jeopardize you or the other rider, or you just aren't in the mood, then don't wave. A nod can suffice, and merely staying on your side of the road and paying attention to where you are going is an equally accepted practice.

good story rather than a bad accident. Deer, of all forest animals, are notoriously erratic, and their movements are impossible to predict. Riders who frequent areas where deer live often view them as "rats" because of the danger they present to moving vehicles.

You're having a great ride through a beautiful canyon area. You have seen only a few cars all day and have been sailing through smooth turns when you come around a corner and are suddenly confronted with gravel sprinkled liberally across the road. Your bike swerves and slides before regaining traction, giving you a genuine *pucker moment*: your whole body seizes up momentarily before you are able to catch your breath and relax your muscles once more.

You're having such a grand time on your ride through a scenic valley that you don't notice the reduced speed sign ahead as you approach the quaint little town. Unfortunately, the local law enforcement agent did. Lights come on, and you realize that you may be about to receive a *performance award*. While you may have some idea of what to do if you are in a car, there are conflicting opinions on how to handle this unpleasant situation while on a motorcycle. I've spoken with patrol officers and read quite a few articles on the subject. One school of thought says to get off the bike and remove your helmet so the officer can see your face and so you can hear what he or she is saying. No, states another source: stay on the bike and leave your helmet on for safety in case you should fall and so the officer doesn't see it as a potential weapon. Still another recommendation is to stay on the bike but quickly take off your helmet. The common thread, however, is to be respectful, to keep your hands visible at all times, and, if you keep your helmet on, to open your visor so the officer can see your face. If you can't hear the officer, ask him or her if you can remove your helmet. Because your registration and driver's license may be in your pockets or in a compartment of

It's not as easy as it looks—holding a bike upright takes strength and balance.

your bike, let the officer know what you are doing before reaching for anything. Hopefully, you'll never receive one of these special citations, but it's always wise to be prepared.

Utilizing the skills that you are continually practicing will help you stay focused when these, and other, unexpected moments inevitably occur. Your goal is to keep them from becoming anything more than quick heartbeat-stoppers, and that is where ongoing training, reading, and mental rehearsals of "what if" scenarios will ultimately pay off. In all of the foregoing situations, knowing how to respond quickly and correctly may make all the difference between a great laugh or a sad tale.

Physical Fitness

Riders do not need to be marathon runners, bodybuilders, or Olympic swimmers to be successful on a motorcycle. People come in all shapes and sizes, and the only real requirement is that you can physically handle the bike that you are riding. However, just like any endeavor, the better shape you are in, the more likely you are to have stamina and the easier it will be to maneuver your bike, particularly if it is heavy.

Are you able to sit for long periods, lift your bike off its side stand on an incline, monitor your fatigue and hunger, and do everything else that you need to do to manage your machine? If you are unable to flatfoot your bike (put both feet flat on the ground while seated on your bike), are you able to balance it comfortably, holding it upright confidently no matter the surface? If you are interested in track riding, are you able to move easily from side to side on a speeding motorcycle with your knees bent tightly while your torso hugs the gas tank? On dirt, can you stand on the foot pegs and balance the handlebars over rough terrain while keeping your head up and your eyes forward? If you're a long-distance rider, do you have the stamina to pound out mile after mile, often day after day?

When I first became involved in long-distance riding, I had no idea of the physical demands that it would place on my body. Whether as pillion or as rider, I found that strengthening my core muscles helped fight pain and fatigue in my back and neck. Lifting weights increased my arm strength, enabling me to more easily maneuver my bike manually, particularly when I needed to move or park it on uneven surfaces. Training to run half-marathons prepared me for the physical and mental demands of a multi-day riding event as I learned how to manage my emotions and thoughts over long periods of time. While starting or maintaining a complex fitness program certainly isn't necessary to be a highly accomplished motorcyclist, anything you can do to build confidence in your body's ability to handle whatever situations may arise will be advantageous to you as a rider.

I usually ride a BMW R1200 GS Adventure, but one day I borrowed a friend's 250 Rebel to ride to work just for fun. I wear a one-piece red Aerostich Roadcrafter suit and an Arai full-face helmet with a very bold graphic on it, and I'm almost 6 feet tall, so I know that I looked pretty silly on the tiny bike. As I waited at a stop sign, a woman on a Suzuki SV650 pulled up next to me. I looked over at her and gave "the nod." She nodded back, but I could see her shoulders shaking with laughter. She thought I was a joke, assuming that I was some kind of wannabe out on a beginner's bike. Another time, I rode a 400cc scooter and led a few riders on a twisty road. One guy came up to me afterward and said he that could barely keep up with me and had scraped his center stand going around one corner. I could tell he was shocked that a scooter could handle the curves like that. I just smiled and told him, "It's not about the bike."

Chapter 5

Important Purchases

The right bike for you is the one that you feel comfortable driving.

he lecture portion of my MSF class took place in a seminar room just off the main showroom floor of a motorcycle dealership. During breaks, I wandered around, checking out the different styles of bikes and sitting on ones that intrigued me. In class, I was riding a Honda Rebel, a small 250cc, easy-to-handle bike. I liked how comfortable I felt and how in control I seemed. I wanted something a little bit larger for my first purchase, however, and was drawn to the Honda Shadow. It had a low center of gravity, it was fairly lightweight, and it was easy for me to get my feet flat on the ground when I stopped, so it seemed perfect for a beginner. However, I also knew that it was not the right bike for the type of riding I intended to do in the long run. I wanted to ride long distances, and for that style of riding, a more upright touring bike would be most appropriate. What to do?

My husband encouraged me to go for the long-term bike, and I listened to him instead of my gut instinct. I bought the motorcycle that I might want once I was a confident rider, not the beginner bike that would instill that confidence. Instead of falling further in love with riding, as I expected to do after having so much fun in the class, I was falling off my new bike at simple stops. I was unable to get my feet stabilized by standing only on my tiptoes, and the top-heavy bike instantly punished me if I was even slightly off-balance. Reacting to my fear, I sold that bike and purchased the Honda Rebel, secure in the knowledge that I could handle it without a problem.

Now, although this bike was easy for me to handle, it was not the bike for venturing much farther than around my neighborhood, with its limited power and small size. I felt silly putting on all my gear only to putter around the block, yet I wouldn't go anywhere without it on. When I needed to run to the store, I grabbed the car keys instead of the bike keys, and soon I was once again looking for a buyer on Craigslist.

Feeling a bit like Goldilocks, I finally found the perfect fit for me when I was willing to listen to my gut and purchase a training bike: one that was big enough to take me onto the freeways as well as back roads, building my confidence as I covered miles. I started to enjoy riding again: I was excited by daytime rides with girlfriends and to be gradually increasing my range until I was ready for my first long-distance trip. Taking the longer ride convinced me that not only had my days as a pillion come to an end, but that it was time to commit to a larger bike that was better suited to my current, as well as future, riding needs. I took the time to "try on" many different models over several months, and I finally chose the bike that I currently ride. While this one allows me to comfortably handle the long distances I dreamed of when I took my first lesson, it's one of many that I imagine I ultimately will own.

International Motorcycle Show

The International Motorcycle Show is an annual event that tours various venues across the United States, bringing together a wide variety of motorcycle brands under one roof. These shows are typically spread over three-day weekends and often occur during the fall and winter months, when riders are starting to get itchy staying indoors instead of being out on the road. In addition to the motorcycle manufacturers' showcasing their newest and most popular models, there are vendors displaying full ranges of accessories, gear, gadgets, and other useful items for riders of all skill and experience levels. In addition, touring companies, riding schools, rider organizations, and other rider-oriented services have booths where you can stop in and chat. Attending one of these events is a great way to become immersed in the biking culture and gather a lot of helpful information. To learn more or to look for show locations and dates, check out www.motorcycleshows.com.

*Attending a motorcycle rally or
exhibition will give you an idea of just
how many options are out there.*

What's the Best Bike for Me?

Many factors go into selecting your first motorcycle. Do you spend hours reading magazines, daydreaming about the kind of riding you want to be doing, or do you simply have a desire to learn to ride with no idea about the variety of ways there are to express that desire? Have you imagined short daytime rides or high-speed turns on the track? Are you in need of inexpensive transportation to commute to work, or are you gearing up to complete your first 1,000-mile day? Have you been itching to join your friends off-road, barreling along old Forest Service dirt tracks, splashing through streams, and dodging rocks and fallen trees? Do you envision yourself as a "wrench"—someone who wants to tear down and rebuild a vintage bike that you can then putter around on—or would you prefer a shiny new motorcycle that comes complete with a service warranty? Knowing what you require in a bike will help you narrow down your choices to those that are most appropriate for you.

But if you aren't sure yet, there's no need to worry. No matter what approach or style of riding describes you, your early steps really should be the same; unless you know exactly what you want, you will typically choose a training bike for your first bike, the one you will use to improve your skills and gain confidence. It's helpful to see your first bike as the one you will pass on to another new rider when you're ready for your next motorcycle. It's also OK to change your mind after you spend time on a new bike, learning more, meeting other motorcyclists, and figuring out the direction you want your riding to take you.

Talk with a reputable motorcycle dealer and ask questions regarding different models and their uses. Talk to friends who ride and find out what they like about what they do. Read magazines, blogs, and online forums or watch videos of other riders to start you on a path of discovery. Gathering all the information you can will help familiarize you with what's out there and what you need to know.

Motorcycle Styles

When I was first introduced to motorcycles, I assumed that a bike was a bike was a bike. Of course, I'd seen different makes and models on the road, but I'd paid little heed to the wide variety of styles available and what the different types of bikes could be used for. It didn't occur to me that there was a reason for having more than one motorcycle in the garage other than to fulfill a love of machinery. However, as my knowledge of motorcycling grew, my appreciation for the different varieties increased and so did my desire to have more than one bike. Now, when I am confronted with buying a bike, it's hard for me to decide on the perfect one that comprises everything I want and can handle all the potential scenarios that I may encounter. I want a bike that can venture down dirt roads to remote campsites, one that is heavy enough to handle the elements on long-distance trips, and a lighter, more nimble bike for zipping around local roads. What's a girl to do?

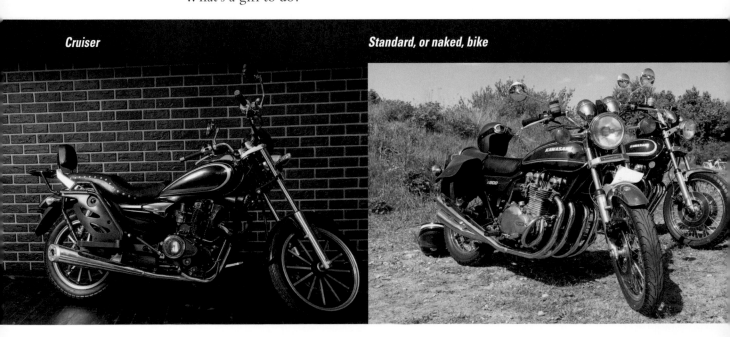

Cruiser

Standard, or naked, bike

Motorcycles are typically grouped by their intended use, seating and leg positions, degree of fairing (protective shielding), and number of wheels. The most common categories are cruiser, standard (or naked), touring, sport, dual-sport, dirt bike, scooter, Spyder, and trike. Several manufacturers extend categories even further, such as sport touring—a blend between a sport and touring bike—and many riders add sidecars to a traditional two-wheeled motorcycle making yet another subcategory.

Cruisers have a low center of gravity, with the rider's legs forward and arms typically higher, resulting in an upright or slightly reclining seating position. Many manufacturers offer cruisers, but Harley-Davidson is the most recognized brand for this style. Because cruisers are lower to the ground, they often have less clearance for high-speed cornering, but riders with shorter inseams are able to flatfoot these bikes with ease. The seating and leg positions can make it a bit challenging for new riders to maneuver the bike at low speeds, but the gearing and low center of gravity can offset those concerns. There are certain models that are recommended for novice riders, with some believing that their lighter weight or lower seats are better suited to beginners; however, it's really the handling of the bike that can make the greatest difference.

Standard (naked) bikes are often the most comfortable for new riders, featuring foot pegs underneath the body and handlebars in an upright position, designed to keep pressure off the rider's wrists and arms in a natural seating position. These bikes are referred to as "naked" due to the lack of fairing or added plastic; it is a basic bike, and it exposes the rider to the elements. You can add aftermarket luggage to increase the bike's versatility, permitting you to carry extra gear or pick up a few necessities at the grocery store on your way home from work. Standard bikes are great to learn on

Sport touring motorcycle

Sport bike

Dual-sport bike

Dirt bikes

because they come in a wide variety of engine sizes, they lack plastic parts that risk breakage if you drop the bike, and they are lightweight and nicely balanced, making it easy for you to focus on riding.

Touring motorcycles are designed to do what their name implies: take the rider for long-distance rides and do so comfortably. Within this category are sport touring bikes and luxury tourers. The primary differences have to do with the level of add-ons, seating position, and performance capabilities, with the sport tourer's emphasis on performance. A sport touring bike is designed to offer the features that riders want on longer trips without giving up the fun factor of a sport bike. It will typically have partial fairings, a lower windscreen, smaller saddlebags, and a more forward seating position. The luxury tourer has a full fairing to protect the rider from the elements, an upright seating position, and large, fully integrated saddlebags for carrying gear. It normally offers a high, adjustable windscreen, is shaft-driven (rather than chain- or belt-driven), and can carry more fuel with its larger tank. As a result of all these features, the luxury tourer is often heavier and harder to maneuver at low speeds, and it may be subject to more damage if it tips over. Touring bikes may not be the best choice for a beginner; a very reasonable, and often less expensive, alternative is to add saddlebags to a standard bike until you've developed the skills and confidence to tackle a larger motorcycle.

Sport bikes are made for speed, designed to be quick and agile whether on the track or the road. The seating posture is very forward, with your body lying over the gas tank and your feet tucked up and back underneath you. Because of the sport bike's special positioning, it's important to learn to ride correctly to minimize the pressure on your wrists and knees; most sport bikes are not comfortable for longer distances. Sport bikes are very streamlined, and most have either minimal

Scooter   **Trike**

windscreens or none at all. Several manufacturers now make starter sport bikes between 300 and 500cc: lightweight, nimble, easy to maneuver, and fun to ride.

A **dual-sport** motorcycle is built for both on- and off-road riding. Typically lighter in weight than a traditional street bike, it handles well for a weekend of trail riding, yet you can ride it to work on Monday. A dual-sport bike is higher than many other types of bike to give clearance on dirt, and it has few parts that can be damaged should you drop it. These bikes are also popular with many long-distance riders due to their comfortable upright seating position, the ability to add saddlebags and carry camping gear, and their performance in a variety of road conditions. However, they do not offer as much protection from the elements as touring models do because they lack fairings. Dual-sport bikes come in a variety of sizes, many of which are similar in size to the bikes used in basic rider courses, which provides a great opportunity to transition from novice to competent motorcyclist.

A **dirt bike** is exactly what its name implies: a bike made to be ridden on dirt. Lighter, taller, with no fairings or saddlebags, and equipped with knobby tires, it can take you on Forest Service roads, trails, and hill climbs. Because they lack mirrors, turn signals, and horns, dirt bikes are not designed for on-road riding, but a dirt bike can be great for learning the skills necessary to be an excellent off-road rider before transitioning to the streets on a more traditional motorcycle.

Scooters have been gaining in popularity, particularly for driving in cities, where their small size and nimble handling make them good choices for commuting and parking. They are fully automatic and typically have smaller engines, full plastic coverings to decrease noise and wind resistance, and a step-through seating position. The wheels on scooters are smaller than those on

Spyder   **Motorcycle with sidecar**

motorcycles, which can cause wobbling sensations at freeway speeds, and only some of the larger models have ABS braking systems. One model, the Piaggio MP3, has a unique approach to styling, with two wheels close together in the front for added stability. Scooters range in size from 50 to 650cc, and the weight, handling, and maneuverability of each type can vary greatly. Although learning to ride on a scooter can build some skills, not all techniques translate to riding a motorcycle due to wheel size, the lack of a clutch and shifting, and differences in steering and overall handling.

There are two styles of motorcycle with three wheels: **trikes** and **Spyders**. Trikes, which are converted from standard motorcycles, have two wheels in the back, whereas Spyders are specifically designed with two wheels in front. Trike conversions are most frequently seen on Harley-Davidsons and Honda Gold Wings. Many riders choose one of the three-wheeled options for stability. In most states, any style of three-wheeled vehicle requires a specific license because the handling is quite distinct from that of a traditional motorcycle.

Sidecars can be added to a wide variety of motorcycles. They are often added for stability or to carry passengers, pets, or additional gear, but many enthusiasts simply enjoy the "coolness factor." Sometimes nicknamed "rigs" or "hacks," sidecars are made by numerous manufacturers in a variety of styles to meet the demands of the market. Depending on the manner in which the sidecar is attached to a bike, it may or may not lean with the bike as it turns. One company in particular, Ural, has brought back an old Russian design that combines the motorcycle with the sidecar from the get-go rather than offering the sidecar as an add-on. As with the three-wheeled bikes, riding with a sidecar requires specialty training to deal with the unique handling of the combined vehicles.

Purchasing Your First Bike

The excitement of purchasing your first bike can compete with feelings of being overwhelmed by the choices available. Giving thought to style, intended uses, and whether you want a new or pre-owned bike will steer some of your decisions, but one of your biggest considerations may be financial. When thinking about purchasing a motorcycle, it's important to include all of the costs involved in riding. Protective gear, ongoing classes, maintenance requirements, insurance, and fuel consumption will factor into your budget in addition to the initial outlay for the bike. Remembering to factor these in at the beginning may help lessen the sticker shock and prevent you from cutting corners that might jeopardize your safety later on.

Research the cost and frequency of service intervals, which can vary quite dramatically between brands and even between models within the same brand, and estimate your mileage demands to give you a reasonable estimate of the expense of operating your motorcycle beyond the initial purchase price. You don't have to get your bike serviced by the dealer from whom you purchased it; many riders either find local motorcycle mechanics or do the routine work themselves.

Once you have established your budget, it's time to narrow your choices to the type of bike you are interested in. Whether you're buying a new or used motorcycle, a dealership can be a good place to start so that you can see multiple styles of bike in one location. Many dealerships specialize in only one or two brands, so be prepared to visit several showrooms.

What type of bike do you want? It's good to have an idea in mind when you visit a dealership.

A frequent concern voiced by many female riders is that salespeople often do not take them seriously. They describe going into a dealership accompanied by a man and being ignored while the salesperson speaks only to the guy. If, after mentioning that you are the one doing the purchasing, the salesperson's behavior doesn't change, I strongly suggest asking to speak to a different salesperson or taking your business elsewhere.

Some women are completely comfortable going bike shopping alone; one woman described asking her partner to wait outside for twenty minutes before coming in to join her, thus forcing the salesperson to speak with her first. You are establishing a potential relationship with the dealer, and it's important that you are seen as the owner of the vehicle and are taken seriously as a rider. It's OK that you may not know all of the bike's technical aspects; you are still the one who will be riding it, and you are the one who needs to decide which bike is best for you.

Spending time at several motorcycle dealerships allows you to explore the wide variety of bikes available and see which ones fit your body best. Being willing to let go of a particular brand may allow you to find the perfect fit with a manufacturer you never thought of trying. Subtle differences in positioning can make a huge difference when riding. One woman described taking a test ride on two model bikes that were the same except for handlebar positions. "Had I taken a class with the first [bike], I might not have continued; I had no idea how much the handling changed with only that one modification."

While a motorcycle may be labeled "dual sport," for example, the seating, height, and handlebar positioning may be completely different from model to model, and sometimes even within the model itself. As you sit on the different bikes, notice what riding position feels the most natural to you. Some riders prefer leaning over the tank in a very forward angle, some like a more laid-back cruiser style, and still others prefer an upright position. Pay attention to where your arms are: handlebar placements vary widely and will affect how comfortable you are after hours on the bike. Do you prefer your legs tucked back behind you, more directly underneath you, or stretched out in front of you? Put the bike on the center stand so you can put your feet on the pegs to more closely experience what it will feel like when you are actually moving. All of these considerations will make a huge difference as you ride.

A great website for visualizing different bikes and seating ergonomics

Establishing a Budget

Regarding gear, buying some items used, such as outer protective garments, can help stretch your dollars. If you imagine yourself fully decked out in stylish leathers, add that into your initial outlay.

I knew I wanted a Harley, but I was intimidated going to the dealer by myself. The bikes are heavy, and I was afraid I'd drop one and look like an idiot. It helped when the salesperson was a woman who turned out to be a rider herself. She shared her own stories of getting started and gave me the confidence that I needed. She kept encouraging me, telling me that if she could do it, so could I. It really helped talking with another woman. I don't know that I would have felt as comfortable with a man; I might have even left the showroom without talking to anyone.

is http://cycle-ergo.com. You start by scrolling through all the motorcycle manufacturers and selecting models that interest you. Next, you enter your height and weight, and the motorcycle ergonomics simulator shows you what your body will look like on that type of bike—if you will lean forward or sit more upright, if your feet will be underneath you—and give you a general idea of what to expect when you are in the showroom.

A common assumption is that being able to flatfoot a bike—meaning that you are able to get both feet flat on the ground when stopped—is essential. What is actually more important is being able to comfortably balance a bike at a stop no matter the terrain. Bikes have different centers of gravity. Some bikes are very low and can feel quite stable even though they are heavy, while others have a much higher center of gravity, making them feel tippy, especially at low speeds or when stopped. Even on bikes with similar centers of gravity, different weight distributions can affect how balanced they feel.

Do not assume that just because a bike is low, it will be easier to maneuver. The length of the wheelbase, the distance between the front and rear tires, and the positioning of the handlebars affect the weight of the bike as well as the handling. When trying different bikes, hold each one upright and gently lean it from side to side to see if it naturally wants to rest in the center or if it takes a bit of effort to keep it balanced. Sitting on several styles will help you understand what this feels like so you can discover what feels right for you.

A dealer should permit you to take a test ride, which is necessary to discover how the bike feels when moving and how comfortable you are handling it at both low and high speeds. Before you leave the lot, take a few minutes to make sure that you know where all of the controls are and that you can navigate them without looking. Once on the road, use the brake and clutch to see how responsive they are before you head into traffic. Ride on side streets as well as busy streets, making right and left turns and going around curves. If possible, take it on the freeway to see how it handles. Is it smooth or thumpy? Does the wind pressing against you bother you, or does the windscreen deflect it effectively?

Is the seating position comfortable in all conditions, and can you easily maneuver the handlebars? Is this a motorcycle you will take to a parking lot so you can spend time practicing U-turns and pulling into tight spots as you build your confidence? Can you imagine going out for regular rides on this bike, honing your newly acquired skills and having fun?

Before you buy any bike, make sure that you can comfortably sit on and balance it.

As you return to the dealer, notice how easy or difficult it is to navigate the parking lot. Most bikes are easy to handle at speed; the crucial test is how you feel when going slowly. No matter how great the bike may look, it is essential to be absolutely sure that it fits you.

Knowing ahead of time how much you are willing to spend can assist you with creating a purchasing strategy before you have to deal with the pressure of

The best bike is the one that fits you: fits your body, your riding style, and your intended uses. What works for someone else will not necessarily be the right bike for you. Friends come in all shapes and sizes, clothes come in all shapes and sizes, and motorcycles are no different ... listen to your inner voice and take your time. Find the one that feels right, the one that you'll want to pull out of the garage and ride.

Some dealerships feature multiple motorcycle brands.

negotiations. Shop around to find good deals or salespeople who offer reasonable prices. Be willing to walk out the door if the dealer or price doesn't feel right. The markup on new bikes isn't as high as is often found in other industries; dealers profit from creating loyalty in which the customer returns to purchase gear or comes in regularly for routine service. Nonetheless, it's reasonable to expect some willingness to negotiate. For example, if you are planning to buy your bike and gear from the same dealer, you may be able to get a significant discount on your accessories in lieu of a lower price on the bike itself. Much will depend on the popularity of a given model and the flexibility allowed by the manufacturer of the bike. My philosophy is that it never hurts to ask!

Experienced female riders assume that they will need to make some modifications to their bikes to adapt them to their bodies. New riders may not be aware that such changes can be made and that they can make a bike more comfortable or easier to handle. You can often lower a bike's seat or get a custom seat that is softer, harder, narrower, or wider. Women tend to have a shorter arm reach than men do, and handlebars can often be modified to compensate. Be sure to voice any concerns with the salesperson; he or she can often offer solutions or direct you to a more suitable motorcycle. If you really like a particular bike but think it needs modifications to fit you better, take a look online for a forum devoted to that make and model. Such forums often provide discussions about modifications that others have made that may help you in your purchasing decision.

While it may be exciting to ride a brand-new motorcycle off the showroom floor, buying a used bike can be a great way to save money. It may also encourage you to buy the correct size for learning. When you are first starting out, it's

A good fit is unique to every rider.

reassuring to have a bike that you don't mind scratching when you invariably drop it a time or two. Most dealers have an inventory of newer pre-owned bikes. If buying used, especially from a private party, ask to see the service records. Make sure that the VIN number on the registration matches the one on the bike and that the owner has clear title to sell it. Check the ground where it's been parked for signs of leaks and ask questions about anything that seems unusual. Have the bike checked by a mechanic to look for signs of wear, corrosion, misuse, or evidence of accidents, and be concerned if the seller refuses to let you do this. If the bike hasn't been ridden for a long time or hasn't been stored properly, there may be damage that is not visible to an untrained eye. No matter how nice the seller seems or how clean the bike looks, it's always wise to "trust, but verify."

Familiarity with Your Bike

Once you purchase your motorcycle, whether new or pre-owned, spend some time getting to know the ins and outs of how it operates before you take it home. While you may be itching to get on it and go, learning about the details and idiosyncrasies of your specific make and model bike will help you be a more competent and confident rider.

If it's a new bike or a used bike purchased through a dealer, your salesperson will typically go over the bike with you, pointing out where the gas and oil go, where the all hand and foot controls are located, how to start it and how to shut it off, and how to put it on the center stand if it has one. He or she should discuss the recommended pressure for each tire (front and rear tires require different pressures) and the type of gas on which the bike will run best. Find out what the fuel capacity should be. Does your bike have a chain, belt, or shaft drive, and what might that mean in terms of routine care? Ask your salesperson to point out any unique equipment as well. The salesperson will often introduce you to someone in the service department who may go over the manufacturer's suggested maintenance intervals with you. Learn how to check the oil and tire pressure yourself; it's OK to ask questions and take notes. Get your salesperson's contact information for any follow-up concerns you may have.

Once you get your new bike home, practice finding the horn, hazard blinkers, turn signals, and high-beam switches without having to look. Go out at night and see how far your lights shine on both high and low beam. Keep track of your mileage for a while until you know how far your bike will go on a tank of gas. Most modern bikes have warning lights to indicate when you are running low on fuel; become familiar with how much farther your bike will go once the light comes on so you can make it to a gas station. It's your responsibility to know how your bike operates; once you know how it should handle, it will be easier for you to tell when something feels "off."

Familiarize yourself with the controls and gauges.

Helmet Considerations

Will you be wearing a helmet and, if so, what style? While I am a fanatic about never leaving home without one, the reality is that some states have helmet requirements while others do not. Your helmet is the one item that you must always purchase new because it must fit correctly; also, there is no way to tell if a helmet has been compromised by being dropped or in an accident simply by looking at it. Helmets are designed only for single impacts and are no longer considered safe once they have hit the ground with any degree of force.

ATGATT

You have your bike, but what do you wear while riding? This is probably one of the most contentious areas of motorcycling, and it is easy to demonize those who choose differently than you. Many riders want to go without helmets, jackets, long pants, or heavy boots, demanding the right to be free to choose. Others insist on never leaving the driveway without full gear. I've seen riders in gear from head to toe as well as helmetless riders in tank tops, short-shorts, and flip-flops. States vary as to helmet requirements, and none has laws regarding clothing. Various biking cultures have differing ideas as to what constitutes appropriate attire.

At this point in time, for the most part, people can decide what they want to wear. When it comes to gear and clothing, it's important to remember that we all share a love of riding, and criticizing one another does nothing to promote a change of behavior in anyone; in fact, it may cause the opposite effect.

Full gear is the norm for many, but not all, riders.

My riding culture is the long-distance community, where wearing all the gear, all the time (or ATGATT) is the norm. I've met wonderful people who have chosen to ride with far less gear, and it's not my place to tell them how they should cover themselves. What I do suggest, however, is to fully understand your choices with eyes wide open rather than with the "it'll never happen to me" stance.

Statistics show that ATGATT is the best way of protecting yourself if you are unfortunate enough to be involved in any type of accident. Even a low-speed, low-side slide down the road can potentially cause severe enough damage to require skin grafts. Likewise, while you may have a hard skull, the brain underneath it wasn't made to absorb high impacts. It may not seem "cool" to cover your body head to toe with protective gear, but it isn't cool to live with the effects of an unplanned get-off, either. Should you ever get into an accident, you, as well as your family and friends, may be eternally grateful that you chose safety. Unless you are single with no dependents, there are other stakeholders in your coming back home in one piece after each ride. Spending money on motorcycling gear may seem costly, but hospital bills and long-term disability are far costlier.

In college, I dated a guy who purchased a motorcycle for his commute to classes. I never rode on the back with him, and while he enjoyed riding, it wasn't really a passion; it was primarily for transportation to and from school. I remember him coming to my house one afternoon, limping inside and asking for my help. He'd been driving over the canyon roads from one part of the city to the valley and had low-sided the bike when he hit gravel on a curve. Neither he nor the bike were badly damaged because it had been a low-speed fall, but the denim from his jeans had torn, and his leg was scraped up. Tending to his wounds, I was struck by how deeply the material from his pants had embedded into his skin. I recently heard a quote: "Your jeans will give you five seconds of blue before you see red," and I can personally attest to the truth of that statement. That image of denim mixed with blood and torn skin has stayed with me to this day, and it informed my personal decision about what to wear when I began to ride.

I met my husband for the first time at a local restaurant for dinner after a brief online correspondence. I knew that he rode motorcycles, and we talked about them during our meal. Walking out to his bike with him after we finished eating, I watched as he pulled a heavy pair of pants and an equally heavy jacket out of the motorcycle's saddlebags. I asked him about the gear while he suited up. "I always ride covered from head to toe: boots, gloves, protective pants, and jacket, and a full helmet. I won't even go around the block without it. I'd rather sweat than bleed." I thought back on my college boyfriend and his accident, and I imagined the difference that protective clothing would have made. While he still would have been sore and maybe bruised, he wouldn't have scars from the scrapes and road material burns.

When I went for my first ride with Terry on our third date, I borrowed some of his gear to protect my body from the elements and any potential accidents. His gear was a smidge too big, a lot too heavy, and a bit warm for the spring weather. I wondered what it would be like to wear just my jeans, hiking boots, and a jacket, but the image of the denim burns once again flashed through my mind. I kept the gear on. I have never been on a bike without it.

Brittany Morrow was involved in a motorcycling accident as a passenger in 2005 and spent more than two months in the hospital, recovering from her injuries; she needed skin grafts on more than 50 percent of her body. She first shared her experience on SpeedFreak.com, and it has since gone viral. Pairing with the Motorcycle Safety Foundation, Brittany has become a vocal spokesperson for wearing all the gear, all the time. Her vivid story and photographs can be found at Get Your Own Bike (www.getyourownbike.com/BrittanyMorrow.htm) and on the Rock the Gear website (www.rockthegear.org). For anyone considering riding

without protective clothing: please read her story and spend a few minutes closely examining her photos. Make a well-informed decision before choosing to skip the gear. Vanity and coolness are no substitutes for skin.

Accidents are not the only sources of damage to your body: being hit by bugs and rocks at 70 miles per hour hurts. I have actually been bruised through my pants by rocks thrown up from passing cars and by giant bugs slamming against my jacket-protected arms. Imagine the consequences if I had not been protected? Not to mention, prolonged sun exposure dries out and ages your skin. Should you choose to skip the outer gear, at least use moisturizers and sunscreens; the wind can be cruel to women's faces. While it may seem counterintuitive, riding in extremes of hot weather without covering your body actually causes more evaporation and can increase your chances of overheating or dehydrating. Having a variety of clothes to wear for different weather allows you to better adjust to the conditions. In intense heat, wearing the right clothing, keeping it wet inside the correct jacket, and keeping the air from direct contact with your body can actually keep you cooler.

Road rash is the result of skin meeting pavement.

Dressing the Part

What's the best outer gear for motorcycling? It will depend to some degree on the type of riding you intend to pursue. Proper motorcycling leathers provide great protection against the road. They're what you will see on racers who walk away from high-speed crashes and slides bruised but intact. Leather can be form-fitting and sexy, looking far better on many bodies than bulkier materials. However, leather is not waterproof, and if you ever get caught in a sudden downpour, you will appreciate having a rain suit to cover your gear.

If you plan to ride in all weather, you may want to consider some of the high-tech waterproof materials so you won't need to stop under an overpass to don your

"Catching a yellow jacket in your shirt at 70 miles per hour can double your vocabulary in an instant."

—Anonymous

rain gear when the skies appear threatening. Additionally, protective gear made from these materials is designed to absorb impact and protect you when sliding on pavement, with crash pads on the knees and elbows and optional pads for your hips and back. Some manufacturers offer one- or two-piece versions; as a woman, I prefer two pieces for personal hygiene functionality.

The type of riding you intend to do will help narrow your selections. Track-racing gear is different from what is appropriate for long-distance riding, and neither may be right for Sunday group rides. Your motorcycle is a certain brand, but you may find suitable clothing in another dealer's showroom. Harley-Davidson riders often want H-D gear, and dealers provide an extensive array of both street and motorcycle clothing. Some women want pink gear, but others will run in the opposite direction when confronted with what they consider to be "girly" gear.

Everyone may offer you their opinions about what you just "have to have." Take the opportunity to ask questions about why they like their gear, any problems they have had with it, how they use it, and why they believe it is the best for you before taking their word for it.

I found that the right type of jacket depended on where I was planning to sit on the bike as well as the style of bike I would be riding. The length of the jacket made a big difference in my comfort: when riding pillion, a longer jacket ended up pushing the shoulders up to my ears, a very disagreeable feeling when sitting. The same jacket, when riding solo, covered my back nicely as I leaned slightly forward.

Covered from head to toe for an off-road adventure.

Whether riding as passenger or driver, sitting on the bike you will be riding is an important way to discover how the jacket and pants will feel when you are moving, not just when you are standing in the store. Awkward angles in the knees when upright may make far more sense when your legs are bent to reach the foot pegs.

The degree of fairing and the size or lack of windscreen will impact how the wind and weather affect you. Do you tend to get cold or hot easily? Will your pants and jacket provide adequate protection from the elements, or do you need additional gear?

Wind and weather affect the passenger differently than they affect the driver. There is often a "bubble"

With ample fairings and windscreens, these bikes offer significant wind protection to their drivers.

created by the windscreen that diverts the air up and over the front seat, but that bubble does not typically carry over to the back. If riding as pillion, wind and frigid air can blow up against your legs and arms, causing cold spots that need may need additional protection. You are also less active than the driver and may need more layers to compensate. Conversely, due to the proximity of the rider in front of you, you may not get as much air circulation on hot days. Consider all these factors when purchasing your clothing.

When looking at outer gear, take the time to investigate different brands and styles. Women's gear has been slowly evolving, and manufacturers are starting to address the reality that the female body is not simply a shorter version of a man's. Be prepared, however: the selection of clothing available for the motorcycling market in general is small, and it's even smaller for women. There aren't enough riders of both sexes combined throughout the world to warrant manufacturing the volume necessary for every person to find the perfect style and fit. You will not find the variation of shapes and styles that you may have come to expect when shopping for street clothes, but what's out there has improved dramatically. If you are willing to be diligent and flexible, you can find clothing that fits and is available in colors other than pink or black.

American and European clothiers tailor their products to different body shapes, so trying on similar sizes in different brands may lead you to a better fit. There are a few companies that make custom suits, but be prepared for the additional cost. Dealers may be limited in showroom space and selection, and it may be tempting to try something on in the store only to purchase it online. If you find what you want in the store, support the store by purchasing it; however, if you

It is important that gear fits well; if it is too big or too uncomfortable, you will tend to avoid grabbing it when you are just "heading out for a short ride"—and it will not be able to protect you if you are not wearing it. Accepting some of the limitations of the available gear for women may be frustrating, but going without gear may be far worse.

can't find what you want at a dealership, check out options online. Gear Chic (www.gearchic.com), a blog devoted to women's riding gear, is a good resource for detailed information about styles, materials, and fit.

A recent study demonstrated that the greatest value of personal protective gear in motorcycling accidents was in lower-energy crashes, ones that do not result in catastrophic injuries or death. In other words, protective gear is most effective in situations that an average rider is most likely to experience: a low-side slide at a reasonable speed of perhaps 35, not a screaming end-over-end crash while racing at 170 miles per hour on the track. The protective qualities of the gear derive from several sources. The material itself provides the first layer between you and the ground and is designed to cover your skin in the event that you slide down the highway. Leather is the most effective against abrasion, with textiles such as Kevlar, Cordura, and SuperFabric coming in right behind. Mesh fabrics are the least protective in a sliding situation, but they offer more protection than T-shirts or denim jackets.

Look for suppliers that carry gear made for women.

The second and most important form of protection comes from the padding typically found inside the shoulders, elbows, knees, hips, and sometimes back of a jacket. Referred to as armor, this padding protects your body from the damages caused by impact. Wearing any kind of motorcycling jacket without the armor, although providing abrasion coverage, has been shown to be ineffective in protecting against such injuries.

There are several types of armor on the market. Different manufacturers use different methods for covering the most vulnerable parts of your body. Foam, whether open- or closed-cell, is the least expensive material used in armor as well as the least protective; in some instances, open-cell foam can absorb water and become useless until it has dried out again. Memory foam, however, is considered more protective, and it rebounds to its original shape after being compressed. Plastic armor provides a hard surface that is often molded to fit the contours of shoulders and elbows but by itself is not particularly useful. However, combined with a foam lining, it is quite resistant to abrasion and impact. Newer materials, such as viscoelastic, are soft and pliable until impact. The armor absorbs the shock of the impact and spreads it over a broader surface, dissipating the energy and, therefore, the potential damage from the blow to the body. The beauty of this material is that it is less rigid and more comfortable inside your gear, yet it is highly protective when needed most.

A look at protective armor on the arms and chest.

Once any type of armor has experienced significant impact, it is recommended that you replace it. You can replace the armor without purchasing a new jacket or pants because the armor is often fitted into specially designed pockets inside the gear.

Motorcycling gear can be expensive. When figuring out your budget, factor in how long and how often you intend to be riding. My Aerostich two-piece Roadcrafter was quite costly, especially when I made a few minor adjustments for an additional price. As a lump-sum purchase, it was hard to click on the "Buy" button. But when I apportion the money over the ten years I know it can last and the amount I ride, plus the comfort of knowing how well it will protect me if I am in an accident, it feels like money well spent. If you are going to wear all the gear, all the time, it's not the place to think about saving a few dollars when it's designed to be saving not only your skin but quite possibly your life.

Consider what you will wear under your protective gear as well. You can wear attractive clothing underneath and step out of your gear when you stop for lunch and socializing. A blogger I know (http://thefashionistahasanironbutt.com) shows up in dresses and heels to long-distance events. She takes pride in being stylish when she steps off her bike and staying protected when on it, putting many of us to shame. However, even she carries her dresses in her saddlebag, opting for practicality and comfort when riding.

No matter what your personal style may be, it's important to notice details, such as where seams hit the seat and if they will they become uncomfortable on a longer ride. Anything that puts minor pressure on your buttocks can quickly become a major irritant in the course of an afternoon. What does your jacket feel like against your skin? Is there a comfortable liner, or will the material become sticky and cloying in the heat? Do the knees and elbows bend naturally when you are seated on a bike? Are your movements restricted at all when you stretch out your arms to reach the handlebars? Will your gear fit easily over whatever you are wearing? If the weather changes, will you be able to add or remove clothing as needed and still fit into your outer pants or jacket? What looks cute and fits well over your t-shirt in the morning may suddenly become oppressive and binding when you need to add a sweater or jacket liner for the ride home in the cool of the evening.

Heat and cold are important factors to consider when purchasing clothing. A lot of riders who live in warmer climates prefer mesh gear, which allows greater airflow while still providing armor in key places. Mesh is not as slide-resistant as other materials, but it is still preferable to shorts and T-shirts. Others use cooling vests; you can place a cooling vest in a freezer overnight or soak it in cold water and then wear it underneath a jacket to slow evaporation as the day warms up. These are great for rides during which the temperatures are expected to soar or the humidity is high. I've occasionally used a neckband that contains a gel that can be soaked in water; when worn around the neck, it provides relief as it slowly dries out.

Motorcycling gloves provide protection and warmth.

After trying various combinations and styles of clothing over thousands of highway miles, I settled on LDComfort (ldcomfort.com) garments, specifically designed for motorcyclists. The shirts and pants I wear can be soaked in water and worn damp. The liquid is pulled away from the skin, but the material retains its moisture for quite a long time, slowly evaporating while cooling the body. However, for short trips around town, I simply put my protective gear on over whatever street clothes I'm wearing and throw my change of shoes into my saddlebag. I still won't ride anywhere without my boots.

There are several ways to stay warm when riding in the cold. While layering works for a quick chill on a short trip, heated gear is best when the temperatures really drop or when you will be out for a longer time. Similar to electric blankets, there are vests, jackets, pants, gloves, and socks with internal wiring that heats up when plugged into the power receptacle on your bike or operated with a battery pack that attaches to your jacket. You can adjust the heat level with a controller. Again, if you plan to ride in all temperatures, make sure that your outer gear will accommodate the added layers comfortably.

When it comes to gloves, spending more often gets you more: more protection, more comfort, and better fit. Good motorcycling gloves will have double stitching that holds together when sliding, strategically placed seams that won't hit pressure points when you grip the throttle or clutch, and hard shells on the impact surfaces. Research has shown that motorcycling gloves that don't have armor provide the same protection as any glove that has not been designed for riding; the armor is essential for preventing serious injuries—but, again, wearing something is always preferred to wearing nothing.

When purchasing leather gloves, make sure that they fit snugly at first; they will stretch as you wear them. Try on any potential purchases while sitting on a

Protection Standards

A standard for armor, Certified European (CE), has been widely adapted to help purchasers understand the level of protection that their gear is rated to provide. This standard is based on energy absorbency upon impact, the most common form of rider injury. The designation EN1621-1 is used for shoulder, elbow, and knee pads, whereas EN1621-2 is limited to the back-protection rating. A CE rating without the numerical codes may indicate that the gear is for use in a sport other than motorcycling. While manufacturers are not required to meet the CE standard, more riders are looking for this seal of approval.

motorcycle and using the brake and clutch. Good riding gloves will often have a slight bend in the knuckles, mimicking the position they will be in when you are holding the handlebars. It's critical that your gloves feel comfortable when you are riding for hours.

Gloves range from minimalist perforated styles for warm weather to fully padded winter-warmth varieties. Most riders have several pairs for different conditions, changing as needed as the day progresses from cool in the morning to warm in the afternoon and back to cool in the evening. Depending upon where you live, you may want different gloves for the different seasons. If you live in a climate where sudden rains tend to spring up, or if you plan to regularly ride in all weather, consider purchasing three-fingered gloves made of waterproof materials that you wear over your regular pair to keep your hands dry in heavy rains. Try them on with the ones you intend to use underneath to make sure that they will fit and that you can get them on and off easily with your inner gloves already on. Again, grip the handlebars to make sure that your hand will move sufficiently to operate your bike. You don't want to be out on the road in a heavy rain only to discover that your fingers won't bend.

Boots serve two main purposes: protection for your feet and ankles, and the ability to stabilize you and the bike when you are stopped. A simple tip-over can catch your ankle underneath in an awkward angle, causing sprains or even breaks. Gravel, oil, rain, and uneven surfaces demand soles that have enough friction to hold you steady when you put your feet down at a stop. Boots can be stylish while still providing full protection, and women of shorter stature often look for ones with thicker soles to add a bit of height. Choose boots that are designed for motorcycling, that go above your ankle, and that have good-gripping soles. Make sure they can easily fit on the foot pegs and that you can shift without impingement. Check to see if laces, hooks, or decorative flairs will get caught on the pegs or your side stand.

Armored boots are worth the added cost if you can fit them into your budget; if not, work boots or hiking boots that cover your ankle are a less expensive

I needed to move my bike a short distance from the gas station to the fast-food place just across a tiny side street. I decided to leave my gloves on top of my tankbag because it was such a short distance. It figures—I hit a patch of gravel while avoiding a large pothole backing my bike into a parking space, and down I went. I must have smacked a rock when I fell because my hand began swelling almost immediately. I know that if I'd had my gloves on, I'd never have felt the hit nor had the injury.

The higher the boots, the more protection they offer.

alternative and preferable to wearing anything lighter or lower. If you intend to ride in all weather, a waterproof boot may be worth the investment. Trying on several brands will help you find the best fit and the most comfortable boot for your riding style. Bring the socks you will be using when you shop, and spend time sitting on a bike, mimicking the different riding positions. Make sure that the boot fits without your foot sloshing around. If you will be riding in colder weather and using either heated or winter socks, or adding a hot pack for warmth, make sure that there will be ample room to accommodate the added thickness without compromising warmer weather fit.

Head Coverings

I won't go anywhere without a full helmet. I've heard too many stories and read too many statistics and reports about what can happen in an accident. The Insurance Institute for Highway Safety reports that helmets have been shown to be effective in preventing approximately 37 percent of deaths and 67 percent of brain injuries in motorcycling accidents; these are both significant enough numbers to warrant serious consideration when taking up riding. But the reality is that states vary as to helmet requirements, and those that do mandate helmets require only minimal coverage. Deciding your level of comfort with risk is the first step in helmet shopping, and the next things to consider are price, fit, weight, visibility, ventilation, and comfort.

Pricing for helmets varies widely, and there are styles available for every budget that meet industry standard ratings. There are two rating systems used in the

United States. Many motorcyclists have strong opinions as to which system is better and which will provide the greatest coverage in an accident. It can be a bit confusing to decide which helmet to purchase based on these ratings because not all helmets meet both standards (although many do). Cost should not be the deciding factor when choosing which helmet is safest; do your research on how you intend to ride and what type of helmet will best meet your needs and budget.

The US Department of Transportation (DOT) has set a minimum standard based on a helmet's shock absorbency that must be met for states that require helmets approved for street riding. The Snell Memorial Foundation created its own standards, which until 2013 were primarily based on shock-resistance capability; they moved toward a shock-absorbency standard in 2013. To add to the mix, there is a European standard, the ECE R22-05, which is recognized worldwide and is required for use in more than fifty countries; it seems to be more closely based on the DOT criteria.

Helmets come in many styles. A simple cap style, or half helmet, will meet the letter of these laws but is not meant to provide the same level of protection as a full-face model. A cap helmet covers just the top of your head and is held on with a simple chinstrap. Your neck and face are exposed to the elements and in an accident. Because this type of helmet doesn't deflect the wind, you can become more easily fatigued.

Some helmets allow you to express your feminine side.

However, wearing a half helmet provides more protection than not wearing one at all.

Three-quarter helmets fully shield the head but do not provide coverage for the face. In a frontal slide, this helmet will not keep the road from contacting your chin, nose, eyes, or skin. While it doesn't protect you from the rain, it does offer more visibility than the full-face models. Some have visors; if not, adding eye protection in the form of glasses or goggles is highly recommended to keep dirt, bugs, and wind from impairing your vision.

A full-face helmet with visor.

A modular helmet adds a flip-front to the three-quarter style; this is a solid bar that covers the chin line but can be lifted up and opened. This model increases the protection for the face, although it is still possible that the bar might flip up or off in an accident. A modular helmet offers greater ventilation because you can lift the chin bar when stopped to cool off for a moment on a sweltering day.

The greatest protection and safest choice is a full-face helmet, on which nothing opens except the visor. Full visors shield you from the elements, including wind and rain, offering a quieter ride.

Several manufacturers have added an internally mounted shaded visor for on-road riding that can be flipped down in sunlight and pushed back up in shade. Having previously owned a helmet that required me to stop and manually change visors from clear to tinted, I highly recommend the flip variety, particularly for rides where you may be frequently moving from shadow to sunlight. Although sunglasses offer protection, the difficulty of quickly removing them and putting them back on as the light changes makes them less useful and potentially a bit more hazardous when riding.

Motorcyclists primarily interested in off-road or motocross riding may choose a helmet designed to meet the specific challenges of riding on dirt and over obstacles. These helmets have a full face with elongated chin and visor portions to allow for more airflow and to give room for wearing goggles.

As with all aspects of motorcycling gear, fit is critical for safety. Helmets have a hard shell covering with an interior liner, typically specialty foam designed to absorb any sudden impact. In some models, the liner is removable, which makes it easier to clean. The fit of the helmet must be snug, almost to the point of the liner pinching your cheeks. However, it is also important that there are no "hot" spots when you try it on. You will find that what hurts a bit now will only hurt more later on, and if it's too uncomfortable, you'll begin justifying to yourself why it's OK to leave your helmet behind (if you live in a state where you have that option). Different manufacturers have different internal shapes, some elongated and some

Put It On!

Learn the proper way to wear your helmet and create a routine every time you get on the bike to ensure that you strap it on securely—it is only effective when it is actually attached to your head!

more rounded. What works brilliantly for your friend may not work at all for you. Ask a dealer to help you find the correct fit for your head. The helmet's weight is another consideration because you do not want to strain your neck to hold your head upright.

Never buy a used helmet, and if you are ever in an accident where there is even a remote possibility that you may have hit your head, replace the helmet—even if there is no visible damage. The protective padding may have been compromised, and there is no way to tell whether that has occurred.

Protecting your hair from sun and wind damage can be accomplished in many ways. Many women simply pull their hair back into a braid. Adding a cloth covering, such as a scarf, bandana, or do-rag, provides more protection for your hair and the opportunity to add a bit of personality and style. Many riders use do-rags under their helmets because they are easy to wash and are often quite comfortable to wear.

Ear protection is essential if you value your hearing. The roar of the motorcycle's engine isn't the issue; it's the intensity of the wind noise that can harm your ears. Many riders use the disposable squishy earplugs that you can purchase at a drugstore, while others have custom molded plugs that are fitted specifically to their ears. Earplugs do not stop you from hearing sounds around you; they simply mute the wind noise. There are also models that connect to your music source, allowing you to listen while riding.

Accessorizing

Depending on the type of riding you intend to do, you may want to consider adding accessories. I'm not talking earrings and purses; I'm talking add-ons for your bike, such as GPS units and Bluetooth communication setups.

A GPS on a bike helps with navigation just as it does in a car. On a motorcycle, if you want to be able to listen to the directions being given, you have to have a way to hear the lovely voice chattering at you. It's therefore a good idea to look into having a communication unit installed in your helmet, thus removing the need to take your eyes off the road to study a map. An added benefit to having a communication system is the ability to listen to music, often through the use of a Bluetooth device, and, should you be with another rider with the same unit, you can sync your devices to talk to each other. None of these accessories is required, however, and many riders opt for the quiet of the road and paper maps, preferring old-school methods to modern technology. For new riders, minimizing distractions until you feel comfortable and competent in a wide variety of situations may be a wise choice. You can always add devices later.

No matter what you add to your bike, accessories should help you focus on riding, not add another level of complexity. I never play music in new situations, in traffic, on twisty roads, or at any other time when I need to focus intently on what I am doing. I let phone calls go to voicemail and check messages when I stop. I even limit conversations with another rider to only what is necessary to get to our location when riding in town or congested settings. Talking on the phone, listening to music, or even responding verbally to a question can have far more serious implications on two wheels than on four. If it takes only a split second for something to happen in a car, it takes half a split second on a bike.

Give yourself time to adjust to any modifications you make to your bike. A GPS voice suddenly talking to you may be startling when you're focused on the road ahead. Looking at the screen may take more of your attention than you realize, and learning how to glance quickly and bring your focus back to the road may take some practice. Knowing the effect of music on your riding is important: is it distracting when you need to be on task? Practice on familiar roads until you are comfortable before venturing out into more complex situations that will demand your full attention. When I first started riding, as pillion, I wanted music on most of the time. I found the more I rode, the less important it became to me; I learned to like the quiet and the places my mind wandered when left alone. Transitioning to riding solo, I carried that with me;

In-helmet systems help riders communcate with the rest of their group.

Your phone suddenly ringing in stereo when you first sync it to your speaker system can scare the hell out of you. When I first hooked up mine, I didn't realize that it would answer automatically, and, out in the middle of nowhere, my daughter was cheerfully yelling, "Hi, Momma!" in my head. I nearly ran off the road.

I still do listen to music, but far less often, and primarily when I am on long stretches of interstate where I find it helps keep me focused when I might otherwise run the risk of getting bored.

No matter the type of GPS unit you choose, unless the manufacturer has integrated it into the bike, you will need a mounting bracket and holder. If you will be riding in areas prone to rain, you'll need either a waterproof unit or a way to protect it from the elements. Mount it where you can see it easily without having to take your eyes off the road for more than a second, where you can still see it in bright sunshine, and where it won't interfere with any other functions on the bike.

Some motorcycling schools offer instruction using Bluetooth communication units, taking you out on the streets and teaching as situations arise. Since my husband and I already used a helmet-to-helmet communication system when I rode pillion, it was natural, when I began riding on my own, for us to talk. He would offer helpful bits of advice in different situation, such as, "When I am passing a semi on the highway, I wait until I know I can get past it and then move to the far side of the lane away from it and pass quickly to make sure I am not caught in its blind spot."

No texting and driving, whether on four wheels or two!

While many of the things he shared I had already figured out from my time as pillion, there were many other times when I would ask questions about how to handle something I wasn't sure of. For example, we were riding on the interstate where a road construction crew had finished resurfacing only one of the two lanes, leaving an uneven lane differential of about 2 inches. On a Saturday afternoon, with the highway almost deserted, it seemed to me to be a great time to learn how to change lanes in those circumstances. I asked for his instructions and then, taking a deep breath, followed them. Success! It was far easier than I had made it out to be in my head, and I felt supported and comforted knowing that he was with me inside my helmet. I learn best in real time and with simple, concise, clear instructions. Being able to communicate easily was, and still is, a fantastic way to continue my learning by asking questions (but he no longer offers unsolicited advice!).

Pay attention to road conditions; you won't always be lucky enough to get a warning.

Packing and Storage Options

Personal Items

Your luggage needs depend on what you do with your bike, how much gear you need to carry, and the kind of weather you may encounter. Even if you never plan to take a trip longer than a hundred miles from home, you may want somewhere to put spare clothing for changes in weather and a few tools for minor breakdowns. Rain gear, extra gloves, and a small tool kit can sometimes mean the difference between getting home quickly or sitting under the eaves of a closed service station for hours, waiting for the weather to clear or for another rider to come along and help you patch the hole in your tire.

Sport bikes are bare bones and typically don't carry a lot of extras, whereas long-distance riders need every inch of space for clothes, heated gear, snacks, spare parts, and water. With some motorcycles, you have the option of purchasing saddlebags and having them added by the dealer; with others, you install them yourself. Most, but not all, saddlebags are removable. Cases come in soft cloth-like materials, leather, or rigid materials such as hard plastic and metal. There are companies that specialize in side bags and others that manufacture top boxes that are attached to the bike behind the passenger seat, which you can install with the mounting brackets that come with them. You can strap a duffel bag onto an empty seat or on a luggage rack.

The first time I went on a multi-day ride with my husband, two-up on the back of his bike, he handed me a very small canvas satchel and informed me

Some bikes come nicely equipped with ample storage.

that I was welcome to bring whatever I wanted, as long as it fit in the bag. My allotted space was three-quarters of one saddlebag; the other quarter would be used for the bike cover. I was clear on what I felt were necessities: a pair of jeans, two tops, clean undergarments, make-up, lotions, street shoes, and a hair dryer. I quickly discovered that my eyes were a lot bigger than my space; there was no way that everything I "needed" would fit. I substituted a pair of lightweight hiking pants for the jeans, brought one top instead of two (knowing I'd be getting a commemorative T-shirt at the event we were attending), packed flip-flops instead of my cuter, but bulkier, other shoes, and ditched the hair dryer in the hopes that the hotel would have one. I wouldn't budge on the make-up. With a lot of shoving and manipulating how things were packed, I managed to cram it all in.

For longer multi-day rides, packing necessities becomes a bit more challenging. It took me a trip or two before I realized that my entire wardrobe did not need to go on a tour of North America, but I did need more items than I would for a quick overnight trip. Over time, I learned to get by with less and to be creative with the space I did have. Now that I am riding my own bike and have more room for clothes, I resist the urge to overpack and continue to opt for items that

> *"Saddlebags can never hold everything you want but they can hold everything you need."*
> —Anonymous

are lightweight and hand-washable, although I still always bring my make-up and throw in a pair or two of earrings. Any article of clothing that can be used for more than one purpose, such as my heated jacket that can be paired with my lightweight raincoat,

Adjusting to Luggage

Remember that carrying extra baggage will alter the feel of your bike, especially if you install it higher up. As always, practice riding in a safe area until you've become accustomed to anything new on your motorcycle.

means one more item that I don't need to find room for and one less satchel to lug into a hotel after a long day of riding. Depending on the length of the trip and the space available on your bike, learning to "get by with less" is often the catchphrase of most experienced motorcyclists.

Some saddlebag models are easily removable and can be carried into your hotel room or to your campsite, but many are not. Several companies sell custom cloth liners designed to fit the interior dimensions of your specific side cases; these can be removed (with your belongings in them) when you stop for the night, leaving the harder outer cases intact on the bike. Specially designed travel clothes that can be quickly washed and dried overnight make a good choice for motorcycling. These clothes are often lightweight and easily packed, and they take up less room than bulkier items, giving you the potential to take along a few extras for variety on a longer trip. Hiking and backpacking gear offer similar options. Plus, most hotels now have blow dryers in their rooms, eliminating the need to carry one if you use one regularly.

First Aid

I am by nature a bit clumsy. I nick my fingers doing the simplest things and find myself reaching for Band-Aids more than I'd like to admit. I have seasonal allergies and can have a sneezing fit if I come across a field of fragrant flowers. While I don't anticipate offering my services as a first responder to an accident, the reality is that accidents can and do happen. Carrying a simple first-aid kit on my bike has come in handy many times, usually when we've stopped to make minor repairs and dinged ourselves up in the process. But I also like the idea of being able to provide a few emergency supplies in the event that I, or one of my riding friends, have a more serious incident. I carry a small backpacking-style kit at all times, tucked out of the way but accessible. I also recommend carrying a bottle of water, sunglasses, and a hat just in case you are stranded alongside the road for any period of time, especially in the heat of summer.

Tools, Spares, and Manuals

Being able to make simple roadside repairs can save you time if your bike should have a minor breakdown when out riding. Knowing your bike is the first step to understanding what tools may be helpful for you to carry with you at all times. Many bikes come with a small tool kit, but if yours doesn't, you can put one together that will address your specific needs. If you live in a city and intend to ride mostly within well-populated areas, you will most likely be able to summon help easily if you break down, but if you are planning to ride in more remote areas, having the right tools may save you hours of waiting for assistance.

No matter where you ride, a tire-pressure gauge is essential for monitoring your tires and keeping them correctly inflated. Having a puncture repair kit and a means to inflate your tires—either an air pump or CO_2 canister—and knowing how to use them will be invaluable for the unfortunate time when you don't see that nail in the road. Spare fuses and headlight bulbs are easy to pack, and duct tape and zip ties come in handy for random, unexpected emergencies. These are just a few of the items to consider having available.

Being able to make some repairs will help in the event of mechanical trouble on the road.

Talk with your mechanic to learn simple repair techniques and how to use the tools you'll have with you. Keep your motorcycle owner's manual on the bike rather than in your garage so you can use it as a troubleshooting reference should something go wrong. If you have roadside-assistance coverage for your car, update it to include a towing package for your bike in the unlikely event that you have a complete breakdown and need to be hauled to the nearest repair facility.

Insurance

States and countries vary regarding their motorcycle-insurance requirements. Although it may be optional where you live, it is highly recommended that you carry it for your protection in case you are involved in an accident. Some insurance companies may also offer discounts for approved training courses, thus potentially reducing the cost to you.

While the following is a private, non-government-affiliated site that can link you to insurance companies for coverage, it also offers a quick glimpse into the standards for motorcycle insurance in each state in the United States: www.dmv.org/insurance/motorcycle-insurance-minimum-requirements.php. I recommend contacting your local licensing agency for confirmation of requirements.

When deciding on coverage, consider the following aspects:

Collision: This will either pay for repairs to your motorcycle if it is damaged in an accident or pay toward the cost of a replacement bike if yours is totaled.

Comprehensive: This will pay for repairs to your bike if it is damaged in a noncollision accident.

Know what your insurance covers in terms of breakdowns and accidents—and hope that you never have to use it.

Medical payments: If you are hurt in an accident, this will typically cover your initial costs until your regular health insurance takes over. It is not designed to cover all potential costs of an injury. Even if someone else is at fault, you don't want to be spending time arguing over bills when you need medical attention; let your insurance company do that for you later.

Towing and labor: This type of coverage will pay for roadside assistance and towing. Some roadside programs for cars can be updated, for additional fees, to cover motorcycles as well. Some motorcycle manufacturers have ownership clubs, such as the American Motorcyclist Association, that may offer towing programs to members.

Medical evacuation: If you are involved in an accident and are unable to ride home, medical evacuation coverage may provide transportation for you and/or your motorcycle. Policies differ, though: some will only transport you if you are an inpatient in a hospital and need to be transported to another inpatient facility. Most will cover the cost of shipping your bike if you are too injured to ride, even if it will not cover your return home. Read the fine print before signing up to make sure that the policy provides the coverage you desire.

Discuss the details with your insurance agent to determine the best type of coverage for your needs. Some policies limit the type of riding you are insured for, and some limit the number of miles you can ride in a twenty-four hour period. You don't want to assume that you are protected only to find out in a time of emotional distress that your policy doesn't provide the help you were counting on.

Chapter 6

Mechanics 101

You don't need to be a mechanic to do routine maintenance work on your bike.

A lthough most riders take their bikes in for routine service and major repairs, it is still important to understand the basic functioning of your motorcycle, how it operates when it is in excellent condition, how to recognize when something is wrong, and how to manage a few simple maintenance issues.

When you first purchased your bike, your mechanic or salesperson may have briefly shown you how and when to perform routine maintenance. But if you are anything like me, you were a bit overwhelmed at the time, and now that you have the bike at home, you struggle to remember the details. The first lesson, therefore, is that YouTube and online forums may soon become your new best friends. Riders are constantly posting videos of how to repair, replace, service, upgrade, or modify almost any part of a bike. Joining online discussion groups for your specific make and model of bike can provide a wealth of information and a place to pose questions as well as discuss what others are struggling with.

If you're interested in becoming a "wrench," or mechanic, and doing more than just the minimum necessary to keep things running smoothly, you may want to start by purchasing the technical service manual for your specific make and model. You might consider taking an "introduction to motorcycle maintenance" course that can familiarize you with basic repairs. Anyone curious about deepening her knowledge or even potentially considering a career as a mechanic should investigate vocational and technical schools for motorcycle-maintenance certificate programs.

"Keep your bike in good repair because motorcycling boots are not comfortable for walking long distances."

—Anonymous

If you're like the average rider, becoming familiar with your bike and its routine service needs may be as far as your interest extends; having your motorcycle ready to get out on the road is your primary concern. What, then, is important to know?

Routine Maintenance

Motorcycles, just like automobiles, require regular servicing to keep them running in top shape. The costs and frequency of routine service can vary quite a bit from bike to bike. This may be an important consideration for you before you purchase a motorcycle, and once you've bought your bike, it's important to follow the recommendations in your owner's manual. Where you bring your bike for maintenance work is entirely your choice; as long as the service intervals meet the stated requirements, your warranty should remain valid. You can choose to do the work yourself, have a mechanically inclined friend help you, take it to an independent motorcycle mechanic, or bring it to any dealer who sells or works on your brand. My bike, as with many makes and models, has an indicator light that comes on to remind me that it's time for service. If yours doesn't, it might be helpful to create a system to remind you when you are due for service—it's easy to forget things that are based on mileage as opposed to visible wear and tear.

Check the air pressure and overall condition of your bike's tires regularly.

Two rubber wheels are all that come between you and the road, which means that they are the only thing between you and many potential disasters. Therefore,

Motorcycle tires come in different widths and with different types of treads for different purposes.

maintaining your tires should be an essential part of your at-home servicing routine. Proper air pressure is a critical component of both tire life and handling. Under- or overinflated tires can wear out more quickly and not perform as expected when you need them to. Check your pressure frequently, have a means of adding air, and know how to do both no matter where you are.

Learn how to measure the tread on your tires; a simple penny will do the trick if you are unable to find or read the wear bars built in to your tires. Stick the coin into the tread—if all of Lincoln's head is visible, it's time to visit the tire store. Visually inspect your tires for foreign objects that may have embedded themselves into the tread, and look at the sides of the tires for signs of bulging or cracking; these are indications that they may be worn and need replacing. It's not uncommon in the United States for your front tire to show signs of wear on the left side before the right. That's due to the natural cant of our roads and riding on the right side of the street. The inside of the tire simply has more contact with the road than the outside. It's also normal for your rear tire to "square off," or flatten in the middle, if you primarily ride on slab rather than twisty roads. But unusual wear isn't normal, and anything that seems odd to you should be checked out.

A motorcycle has one of three main means of propelling the rear wheel: a chain, a belt, or a shaft. A bike with a chain requires frequent routine oiling and adjusting. With some models, you can add an automatic oiler, but in most cases, you will need to learn to oil the chain yourself. Additionally, the chain will stretch with time and mileage; therefore, it's important to check the adjustment on a regular basis and tighten it if necessary. Have your mechanic or service provider demonstrate how to do these tasks, recommend how often they need to be done, and explain any problems you may encounter and how to know if the bike needs additional service. For bikes with belt or shaft drives that do not require the same attention as a chain drive, it's important to know what routine service entails, how often it needs to be done, and how to recognize potential problems.

In some models of motorcycle, the engines are water-cooled; others are cooled by oil or a combination of oil and air. But no matter what they use for cooling, oil lubricates several internal components: the engine, the transmission, and the clutch. Some models guzzle oil; others rarely need additional oil. Water-cooled bikes have coolant; oil- and air-cooled engines don't. Learn how to check all of your motorcycle's fluids and know how to add them if needed; this will ensure proper functioning and prevent damage to your bike. Follow your owner's manual's recommended frequency for changing the oil. Some dealers may encourage changing it more often, but question their rationale; more frequent changes aren't necessary unless you subject your bike to extreme circumstances that may put undue strain on your system. I can't see any reason to spend money on a service that isn't needed, and I imagine you'd prefer to use that money elsewhere!

There are a lot of opinions about what type of oil to put into your bike, whether it is OK to mix brands, viscosity (how it acts in cold and hot temperatures), and types of oils (petroleum, synthetic, or hybrid). According to some tests, higher cost oils, which often have higher quality additives, tend to offer slightly better performance, but even this is not always the case. Research indicates that most major brands of oil are compatible with one another and that no harm will result from mixing them. This can come in handy if you need to purchase oil when on the road and eliminates the need to carry an excess of spare oil. If you will be riding

A close-up look at an engine.

A rear wheel with a chain drive.

Working headlights are a must.

in extremes of heat or cold, use a variable viscosity oil, such as 10W–40 or 20W–50, as specified by the manufacturer. Using a petroleum-based, synthetic, or hybrid oil does not seem to be of significance unless your owner's manual specifically calls for the use of synthetics.

Head, tail, and brake lights can go out suddenly due to a burned-out bulb or blown fuse. Make it a habit to check your operating lights routinely; you don't want to find yourself on a dark highway in the middle of the night with no headlight. A motorcycle's headlight stays on at all times, and it's important to make sure yours is operational; it's one of the few ways that oncoming cars may be able to notice you. Bikes typically have a low beam and high beam, and if your low beam does go out when riding, simply use your high beam until you are able to replace the dead bulb; it's not normally bright enough to offend or blind oncoming traffic if it has been adjusted to aim properly. Knowing how to change a bulb and replace a fuse are important basic skills. Learn where they are located and what tools (if any) you need, and carry spare parts with you. All it takes is one bumpy road and—voilà!—no lights.

Most motorcycle manufacturers recommend more extensive servicing at defined intervals. At these visits, the mechanic will check for worn parts and leaks and will replace items that have an expected expiration date based on mileage. While these maintenance visits can be expensive, the cost of a highway breakdown, towing, and lost time may be more burdensome in the long run. I typically ask to see the parts that have been replaced and have the mechanic point out the worn bits. It's been helpful for me to visualize what I am paying for: even though my bike seems to me to be running just fine, potential problems may be lurking, sight unseen. Worn belts, dirty filters, and gunky oil can't be doing my bike any good. Preventative maintenance, before things break, offers me one more bit of reassurance when I'm out on the road.

An oil and spark-plug change in progress.

Tires

Your bike will come equipped with a set of tires that are typically chosen for your make and model and its expected use. Manufacturers may choose a specific brand because they were able to negotiate a good deal, or they may feel that a specific brand is best for all of their bikes. As a new motorcyclist, whatever comes on your bike will most likely be fine until you learn not only how to ride, but how you ride, what you need, and what you like. As you become more involved with your motorcycle, you'll form your own opinions as to what best suits you; until then, it's best to stick with what the manufacturer believes is best for your bike.

When the time comes for your first replacement set, there are several factors to consider: what kind of rider are you, where do you prefer to ride, how long do you want your tires to last, and what kinds of conditions do you tend to encounter? Buying tires used to be a relatively simple process, but now the number of tires available and advertisements and recommendations about which ones to use can be daunting. Street tires are geared to provide higher mileage on straighter roads, some tires are made for the various weather conditions that touring riders are more likely to encounter, and adventure and dual-sport bikes typically require tires that can be used both on- and off-road. For those who anticipate spending time on the track, there are high-performance tires, and heavier bikes require tires that will safely support the additional load. Within each category, there are even more choices that further refine your ability to grip the road, increase mileage, or simply better match your riding style. No matter what you choose in the long run, it's important that the front and rear tires are made by the same manufacturer and are of the same style so they handle well together.

Worn tires are unsafe and must be replaced.

Many, but not all, new tires come coated with a mold-release compound used by manufacturers during production. Although this makes it easier for the tire to slip out of the mold used to make it, it can cause the tire's surface to be slippery for the first 50 to 100 miles. Tight turns and slick roads are especially challenging until you "scrub in" the new treads. Check with your dealer to find out if your tires have been treated; if they have, take it easy until the compound has worn off.

Tires come in two main shapes or profiles: oval and rounded. Profile refers to where the tires most come in contact with the road. Rounded tires have greater contact with the street surface when the bike is leaned to the side and less when the bike is upright. They are often more wobbly on straight surfaces and can impart a feeling of falling into the turns. If you anticipate spending most of your riding time on twisty roads and leaning into curves and as little time as possible on slab, or flat, pavement, then you may want to consider this profile. If, on the other hand, you see yourself as someone who isn't pushing into twists and turns at full speed, you may want to shop for an oval profile tire. Oval tires have, as the name implies, a more oval shape and increased contact with the road when upright; as a result, they provide a greater sense of stability.

Riders often talk about their tires as being either "hard" or "sticky," referring to how they respond when gripping the road. Different brands and models of street tires have various feels to them as they go through turns and or commute on slab. A sticky-feeling tire may grip the road better, but it will typically have a shorter life span than one that is considered harder and specifically designed for the street. The reason for this difference is the compounds used in manufacturing the tire and the use for which it was made. Racing tires are designed to be very sticky and are built to be used only a few times at high speed under high-heat conditions. As the tire heats up and cools down, the compounds harden and become brittle. Street-riding tires are not subjected to the same temperatures and are made to withstand numerous heating and cooling cycles, making them the preferred choice for the average rider. Sport bikes typically leave the showroom with tires somewhere in between: sticky, but designed for street riding and not the track. To complicate matters further, there are street models that have a harder surface down the middle for better wear while providing a softer, stickier edge for better cornering. This is where understanding what you need from a tire will help you narrow your selection.

Touring and sport-touring bike tires have a different tread pattern than other models. Less groove area equals more tire surface to contact the road, thus more traction and better handling. More tread groove increases the tire's ability to move water off to the sides, thus providing better handling in the rain. Riders who plan to be out in all conditions often prefer this style of tire, giving up some performance in drier weather in exchange for greater safety when the skies open up.

Heavier motorcycles, such as cruisers, need heavier tires to support their weight. Tires for these bikes are

Tire with rounded profile.

Tire with oval profile.

Tires made for racing bikes have a shorter lifespan due to the extreme speed and heat to which they are subjected.

typically made for riding in all weather conditions because most bikers aren't using them for sport. It is, however, important to know the load limits for both your bike and your tires because putting too much weight on either can affect performance and handling and potentially cause serious problems.

Knobby tires are designed for off-road riding, where you need them to maneuver through rocks, soft sand, mud, and gravel while still being able to grip

Knobby tires are better suited to rough and varied terrain.

hard-packed dirt and bits of asphalt. Further delineations within this category include motocross, enduro, dual-sport, and adventure riding. Motocross tires are softer, to help cushion hard landings; enduro tires have stiffer sidewalls, to help protect your rims against rocks and other hard objects; dual-sport tires are rated for the ratio of dirt to street to which they are ideally suited; and adventure tires are for heavier and larger off-road bikes.

Winterizing Your Bike

If you park your bike in the garage for the winter, you need to prepare it for hibernation. Especially in climates where the temperatures plunge into the single digits, proper preparation will prevent unexpected problems when you pull your bike back out in spring. The common elements of winterizing your bike include keeping moisture out of everything, keeping the tires from settling into flat spots, protecting fluids and batteries, cleaning off bugs, and guarding against critter invasions.

Washing your bike before storing it may seem odd, but removing all of the ground-in dead bugs and waxing your motorcycle will help prevent corrosion of the paint and chrome. Leather conditioning on your seat will keep it soft and prevent cracking in the cold air. WD-40 on metal bits will guard against rust. Rubber protector on any rubber parts will keep them from drying out. Plugging the muffler with either a device specifically designed for that purpose or brightly colored (to help you remember they are there) plastic bags will prevent rodents from making a cozy nest inside your bike. Periodically check your bike for signs of infestation. We live on a horse farm, and the mice love to cuddle up near our batteries and occasionally feast on our wiring.

Changing the oil, filter, and other fluids will get rid of anything that may turn to gunk over the winter. Lubricate moving parts and make sure that you have antifreeze in your cooling system if your bike is water-cooled.

Most experts recommend adding a fuel stabilizer, such as Sta-Bil, to prep your gas tank for winter. If left untreated, gas can break down and moisture can get into any air spaces in the tank, rusting it from the inside. Add the stabilizer, top off your bike with gas, and head for home. The full tank and a short ride will mix everything and get you through until spring.

Batteries will slowly drain if left unused for long periods of time. If possible, attach a trickle charger, such as a Battery Tender Super Smart Junior, over the winter to keep you charged up and help extend the life of your battery.

Tires need care as well. Check the pressure and, if possible, store the bike with the tires off the ground to prevent flat spots from forming. A bike stand can elevate

Ready for Spring

Sitting in a garage for a season can subject your motorcycle to moisture, rust, and fluids turning to gunk. It's hard enough to sit out the cold, waiting for spring to come. You want your bike to be ready to hop on and go when the warm weather finally does arrive.

This is NOT what is meant by winterizing your bike!

both tires, but if you don't have a stand, keeping your motorcycle on the center stand will alleviate pressure on the rear tire. If your bike doesn't have a center stand, moving the bike enough to rotate the tires every few weeks will help.

Covering your bike will keep most moisture from getting to it, but use only a cover designed for that purpose. Tarps, while keeping water out, can also trap it underneath, creating an ideal situation for rust to flourish. High-quality bike covers often have mildew protection and venting to ensure the best protection for your machine.

When spring finally does return, recheck all the bike's fluids, take a peek at the wiring to make sure it hasn't become someone's lunch, wipe off any accumulated dust, and start it up to test the battery. When you first get back on, remember that it's been a while since you've last ridden. In addition to making sure that everything is running well, also make sure that your head is back into riding. Despite your eagerness, it's always wise to take it easy for a few miles.

Know Your Bike

When I first started riding solo, I didn't have enough experience with operating any bike to intuitively know when mine might be handling differently than normal. My focus was on keeping it upright, keeping it moving, and making it stop without falling over and embarrassing myself. I was processing traffic, road surfaces, and changing weather conditions and trying to figure out where I was going while still keeping one eye on the whereabouts of my riding partner. As my skills improved and my anxieties diminished, I began to enjoy the bike itself and take more notice of how it handled instead of how I was handling it. I now have opinions about how the tires hold traction in the rain and how much wobble is normal on the gravel road to our house. I can tell when the tires are new and how they feel if they need more or less air. I notice the RPMs and how my riding affects the cooling system. I can tell if any of the levers have been moved too far in or out and what feels just right. I have a good idea how far my low- and high-beam lights should brighten the road at night. I know how many miles I have left when the low-fuel warning comes on and how quickly I need to find a gas station depending on how fast or slowly I am driving. I have become the expert on my bike, and it is my job to notice when it needs attention.

As you become familiar with riding your motorcycle, you will also find yourself getting a feel for how it handles. What's it like weaving slowly around in a parking lot? How does it tackle the bumps and grooves at speed on the freeway? What do you notice about the amount of pressure needed to pull in the clutch or twist the throttle? Does it shift smoothly or need a bit of coaxing? Each motorcycle has its own personality and its own set of quirks. An understanding of your particular bike's nuances will come over time, and as it does, you will also begin to understand and notice when things feel "off."

It bears repeating that, in addition to becoming a safe, competent rider, you must become the expert on your own bike and keep it in top riding condition at all times. To keep your bike a safe means of transporting you wherever you want to go in whatever conditions you may encounter requires vigilance. A slipping clutch, unreliable brakes, or an ignition that becomes fussy and won't start every time are obvious indications that something needs to be checked out; other signs may be more subtle. While you may not be the one to fix whatever is wrong, you do need to be able to explain what you are experiencing to a mechanic. To be able to do this, you must be paying attention! Routine maintenance is the first step; understanding what to do when your bike just feels wrong is a different type of competency—one you should be developing alongside all of your other riding skills.

Knowing your bike means being able to enjoy riding wherever you are.

Chapter 7

Safety

You never know who you'll meet on the road, so be prepared.

Being safe on a motorcycle is more than wearing the right gear and developing your riding skills. It also covers the choices you make about where and with whom you ride, what happens if your bike breaks down, and how to protect yourself should the unthinkable happen and you are somehow involved in an accident, whether as a rider or a witness. It's about being prepared for whatever you might encounter when out on two wheels.

Should I Be Riding Here?

In 2010, my husband and I scouted bonus locations for one of the Iron Butt Rallies. The Rallymaster gave us a list of potential locations where riders would stop, take their photos with their flags, log their odometer readings, and prepare for the next stop before hopping on their bikes and heading off. Unlike riding in the actual rally, where time is of the essence and lingering would cost us points, we were able to take a break, read historical markers, wander through museums, and otherwise enjoy ourselves. Our primary job was to assess each location to ensure that the GPS waypoints were accurate and that there was a safe place at each stop where riders could park their bikes and take their photos. No one wanted a rider to risk an accident at any of the scavenger hunt locations, nor did anyone want riders to be sent to or through places deemed unsafe or unwelcoming.

One location we scouted posed a particular dilemma: if the rider arrived at the bonus at night, he or she would be passing through neighborhoods where drive-by shootings and muggings had been known to occur after dark. Was this bonus, while interesting, worth risking someone's life? No, of course not. But was there a way to mitigate any potential threat while still retaining the bonus? Yes, there was. We recommended to the Rallymaster that she restrict this location to daylight hours only. Most of the streets, although populated with abandoned houses and possibly drug dealers, seemed safe enough to drive through in the middle of the afternoon. The question I asked myself was, "Would I go here if I were by myself, and would I ride through this area at night if I were with another person?" My answer was clear: I'd probably feel safe during the day, but I'd never for a moment consider riding those streets after dark—even if I were with an entire posse!

Stay Alert

All rider courses emphasize that the number-one thing a motorcyclist can do to be safe is to avoid all intoxicants before and while riding. Drugs and alcohol affect your reaction time even when you aren't noticing any of the usual signs of a buzz. Even common, over-the-counter medications, such as cold or allergy drugs, can cause drowsiness and affect your riding. Motorcycling demands your full attention, and anything less jeopardizes your and everyone else's safety. Go for a great ride, park your bike at the end of the day, and then share a toast with your friends.

Those questions form the personal criteria that I use for all of my decisions when riding solo: "Would I go here if I were alone?" "Would I go if I were with someone else?" "Would I feel safe if I were here at night, whether alone or with another rider?" While each rider will answer these questions differently, every woman I've met who rides solo has a similar checklist. We each have our own comfort levels regarding risk, and the considerations extend to more than riding through rough streets at night. Navigating through busy city traffic, turning off onto a hard-packed dirt-road shortcut, joining a new group for an afternoon ride through local back roads, or taking off on a solo around-the-world expedition all demand that you assess what risks might be out there and how willing you are (or are not) to take these risks. What's of critical importance is to know the boundaries of your comfort zone as well as the edges of your personal growth space. Pushing up against those edges can make you a better rider, but bursting through them or ignoring them in the face of pressure from friends and other riders can destroy your confidence and potentially cause you real and serious harm. Whatever choices you make, there are steps you should take to ensure your safety no matter where you go or with whom you are riding.

Staying Safe Alone or with a Group

Whether you're out on the road on your own, with another rider, in a large or small group, or with a passenger, there are different dynamics and different safety considerations to think about beforehand.

Riding Solo

Riding alone, whether in town or off exploring the far corners of the world, carries with it the expectation that you can take care of both yourself and your motorcycle. Clearly, heading to the grocery store by yourself to pick up a gallon of milk carries fewer risks than riding solo down a remote dirt road in South America. However, before you hop on your bike, you need to know that you have a way to solve whatever problem may arise. I often use a variation on the old commercial slogan: I can plan for x, I can plan for y, and for everything else there's MasterCard. It isn't reasonable to plan for every possible situation you may encounter, but there are plenty of common occurrences that you can anticipate and be prepared for. The MasterCard, or back-up, option is having a means of getting additional help when you realize that you need it.

In heavily populated areas, the questions you need to ponder are simpler: Are you able to pick up your bike if it falls, or are you willing to ask for help from a passing stranger? Do you have roadside assistance if your bike breaks down and needs towing? Are you comfortable navigating in busy conditions, finding addresses while listening to your GPS, and searching for a place to park? Is it easy for you to ask someone for information if you get lost? These may seem like basic questions with obvious answers, but they can be major challenges for many new riders who are still mastering the nuances of operating the bike itself. Feeling comfortable with the risks you may face even while close to home will allow you to safely focus on your main task: riding.

For longer trips, or when venturing into more remote areas, the questions become more complex. Are you comfortable coming across people you don't know in isolated areas? Do you have the tools and the know-how to fix the most common issues on your bike at least well enough to get back to civilization and find a repair shop? Can you summon help if you are in an accident

Ask Yourself

Can I handle whatever might happen if I am by myself? Would I feel safe if I were here at night, whether alone or with another rider? Do I have a way of summoning help if something should happen? Would anyone be able to find me if I had an accident?

Your own personal comfort level will determine how far and for how long you want to travel solo.

on a rarely traveled back road? How easily can you pick up your motorcycle if you drop it on a lonely Forest Service road? Does the thought of sleeping in a tent by yourself in a campground of strangers excite you or bring back childhood nightmares of boogey men and zombies? How about staying in a sketchy hotel because all the reasonable ones in the town were booked for a quilters' convention? I certainly have more than my share of "no room at the inn" and "keep all the gear on and don't touch anything while you try and get a few hours of sleep" stories to make me reserve a room ahead of time when riding solo!

While determining your personal comfort zone will dictate your decisions about when to ride by yourself, bringing a few specific items can make your trip a safer one no matter where the road takes you.

A GPS can be invaluable in helping you find your way; it can also be notorious for getting you lost. Mine has sent me down roads that start out perfectly fine only to turn to dirt, gravel, and mud after a few miles. It's tried to convince me that the unpaved road heading straight up the mountain that will save me a tenth of a mile is a much better alternative than the lovely paved highway I just turned off of. It's continuously attempted to have me make U-turns in order to plow through cow pastures. Perhaps a road existed there when covered wagons were a popular form of travel, but the foot-tall weeds and barbed-wire fence isn't inspiring confidence in that route today.

While the GPS unit may be a mixed blessing, knowing how to use one and when to zoom in to see exactly where it's trying to take you are important tools to have. Many smartphones have mapping software in them or apps that you can download, and it's easy to rely on them to navigate for you. Remember, however, that remote areas often do not have good cell coverage, and your GPS application won't work if it can't connect with a cell tower. If you are planning to use your phone as a GPS, it's a good idea to also carry paper maps with enough detail to get you where you are going in the event your phone fails.

A cell phone is a must if riding alone. Being able to summon assistance, call for information, and generally stay in contact with others can be critical if something should go wrong. Even when I want to disconnect from the world, I still have my phone available in an emergency. I can ignore incoming calls, set it to airplane mode, or turn off the ringer; I just want to know that when I need it, I have it. I also have a way to keep it charged while riding so it's always ready to use. Some bikes have USB ports; others have places for car chargers. If yours doesn't have either, you may be able to hardwire something onto your bike using your battery. Find out what your electrical system can handle in terms of extra devices. You can investigate solar cell chargers if you can't tap your bike as a source of power. Whatever you decide, it's important to keep your phone charged. However, it's equally important to remember that it won't work everywhere, and if you plan to ride in remote areas, a back-up emergency system is essential.

Satellite tracking devices are becoming more popular, particularly among solo and long-distance riders. These devices emit signals that can be tracked by others using a link you provide, which can be fun if you want your friends or family to watch your trip in real time. They click on the link and a map appears with dots indicating your route as it unfolds. If you prefer to remain anonymous, however, you can simply keep the link private; this allows you to see your trip later but prevents others from viewing it. But the greatest value of these systems is the ability to call for help should the need arise. Tracking devices typically have two emergency buttons: one for "I'm having problems" and one for "send help immediately."

Most tracking devices require an annual subscription, but if you are considering riding off-road or in isolated regions, the cost may

Riding alone in remote areas means you need an emergency system in place to contact help.

be well worth it should anything go wrong. A friend of mine, who often rides and camps solo, opted to follow her GPS when it presented her with a choice to take a shortcut home from a weekend gathering. Unbeknownst to her when she elected to take this route, the road turned to dirt many miles after she left the main highway. Undaunted, she continued on, figuring she'd get some good off-road practice—although perhaps she was no longer shaving any time off her ride. Her

Stay Alert

Having a few snacks in your top box or tank bag will prevent hunger from affecting your ability to think if you end up riding longer than planned, getting stuck by the side of the road awaiting a tow, or not finding any safe places to stop and eat. Chewing gum is a great way to stay awake and alert after enjoying a leisurely meal that is starting to settle in your stomach and make you sleepy.

confidence grew as she tackled the bumps and gravel until she hit soft sand and the unthinkable happened: a hidden pothole, a sudden lurch of the front wheel, and she was on the ground, her bike trapping and breaking her ankle. She could reach the handlebars to hit the kill switch on her engine, but, more importantly, she found her Spot tracker and pushed the SOS button: send help immediately. The Spot monitoring system was able to locate her position using GPS coordinates and contact the nearest authorities, and help arrived within an hour. Her family met her at the hospital, her ankle eventually healed, and the story had a happy ending. Just imagine the narrative without the tracking device, though: no cell coverage, alone on a dirt road, unable to lift the bike off her leg, and at risk of potential shock from the injury.

Many women I spoke with mentioned having an escape plan: a way to get out of any uncomfortable, scary, or potentially dangerous situation. Gas stops were the most common theme: what if I run out of fuel in a less-than-desirable area? The first recommendation they all had? Plan ahead. Know how far your bike will go and find gas stations in safe locations, even if it means filling up well before you need to. Most GPS units have resources for finding fuel and can tell you where gas stations are located and how many options you have. With that information, you can then decide if you should stop right away or if you can make it a few miles farther to a safer place. Time of day matters as well: what's fine by day may be sketchy at night.

Sometimes, despite the best-laid plans, your choices will be limited. Your only options may be stop somewhere you'd rather not or run out of gas by the side of the road. What you decide is based on your assessment of the risks involved: would you feel better in a rest area or pullout alongside the highway, waiting it out until the sun comes up, or do you feel bold enough to ride into a rough

Whether in a sketchy part of town or on a deserted highway, there is safety in numbers.

part of town at night? Is there a safe place to wait while you call for roadside assistance? If strangers approach you and seem threatening, do you have a plan to get away?

One friend stopped at a service station late at night, unaware that it was a hangout for local gangs. When some guys started to approach her as she filled her tank, she had to think quickly. She knew that with her helmet and gear on, they couldn't tell if she were male or female, and she didn't want to let them come close enough to find out. Returning the nozzle to the pump and closing her tank, she started acting as if she were hearing voices in her head, talking to herself in a deep, manly voice, shaking her fists in the air and kicking at the ground. She pretended she didn't see anyone, and she kept up her act as she got back on the bike and rode away. The gang didn't know what to make of her, and they let her go without incident. Her quick thinking probably saved her from a far worse encounter. Other friends have mentioned pulling into a gas station, feeling an undefined discomfort, and simply pulling back out onto the street without stopping. There may not have been anything wrong, but they have learned to trust their gut instincts, opting to be on the side of safe rather than sorry.

Carrying some form of self-defense equipment may come in handy if it is easy to access and you know how to use it for its intended purpose. Some women carry pepper spray; some have knives that they keep on hand for numerous uses, among them safety; and still others have taken self-defense classes or have learned a martial art. At least some of the protection that all of these provide is psychological: the rider has taken action to defend herself and has some confidence that she can get away from a potential threat rather than being at the mercy of a dangerous stranger or situation. Prevention is the key: know your surroundings, stay aware of everything around you, and make good decisions that work for you. The reality is that while most of the people you meet when riding solo are far more likely to offer to buy you lunch than cause you harm, being unaware and caught off-guard can put you at risk. Therefore, whatever helps you feel confident in your ability to take care of yourself is going to be your best defense.

Riding with Others

Going out for a ride with a group or even one other rider can be a great experience. Camaraderie, not always having to be responsible for planning the route, and the possibility that someone else will know how to repair your bike if you don't are only a few of the positive aspects of joining with others. But riding in a group can also increase your risk of getting lost or having an accident if you don't take certain precautions.

I went on a small group ride not long ago, and I was surprised by the number of women who didn't have a GPS or map, who weren't familiar with the area, and who had no idea how to get where we were going or to get back to our campsite if, for any reason, they got separated from the group. The ride leader didn't review the route or have a contingency plan for emergencies. Although we were headed to a fairly popular destination with signage along the way, there was plenty of potential for us to get split up or for riders to get lost.

By comparison, on an earlier ride with a much larger group, the leader reviewed the directions that she had sent out prior to the gathering and discussed key turns where we'd meet up should we get split up. She shared her expectations regarding each person taking responsibility for her own ride. She reinforced her safety concerns by asking riders to not make the mistake of trying to keep up with others by, for example, rushing through a stoplight as it is turning red. She made sure that everyone had her cell phone number so they could call and leave messages if, for any reasons, they needed to turn back. By a show of hands, she asked new riders to identify themselves and invited them to share their names and comfort level with group rides. She made sure that she answered any first-time riders' questions before moving on. She had assigned another woman to ride sweep, or last, to keep an eye on all the other riders and be available if there were any problems. She demonstrated the hand signals she'd be using, talked about how to ride in staggered formation, and explained how to pass if necessary. Only after making sure that all the riders understood her expectations and rules did she have everyone mount up and head out.

Failing to address the aforementioned issues can

The camaraderie of a group outing is undeniable—just ask the Rainier Ravens.

lead to potential problems when riding with others, especially in a group. Adding to the mix are different riding styles, variable speeds, and a variety of comfort levels regarding how close riders get to other riders' bikes. Group rides can turn dangerous when someone reacts to something in an unpredictable manner, causing others to respond quickly, which, in turn, can set off a chain reaction for those behind. I've seen riders pass on the right and pull into another lane for no apparent reason and then just as suddenly lurch back into the group. I've been behind erratic bikes, watching them slow down to a crawl on curves only to pour on the throttle, often reaching excessive speeds on straightaways. Riders can be lulled into inattention when following others, forgetting to maintain perhaps an even higher state of vigilance than when riding solo. Some may feel the pressure to ride above their ability level in an attempt to keep up with the group, and others may become frustrated by slower riders and thus take risks to pass and get ahead.

To travel safely with others means talking bluntly about how you expect the group to behave and what your role in the group should be. It then includes spending time together to learn about each other and how you ride to see if the group is ultimately a good fit for you. With the right mix of people and the correct expectations,

Having a way to communicate is essential for a group of any size.

group rides can be great experiences, but with the wrong group and the wrong expectations, what you hope will be a lovely day ride can turn into a disaster.

My husband and I ride together all the time; I know how he rides and how he thinks. I've learned from him where I need to be and what to do when confronted with a problem. We come to stops staggered, not next to each other; in the remote chance that one of us slips and falls over, there's no need for both of us to go down. I pull in behind him on right turns, giving me more room, especially if it's a tight corner. I decide where to park when we need to stop, and he navigates around me. We know to look for a safe pullout and wait if one of us gets caught at a stoplight. I can voice-dial him if we somehow get separated so that neither of us has to come looking for the other. A friend and her husband have a different but equally well-understood rhythm when they ride. When she and I first went out together, we had to learn each other's patterns, and we had a few close encounters on the bikes when our styles clashed. Clarifying expectations and verbalizing our intentions has helped us avoid further problems, and we now have a great time when we go on the road together.

Communication, therefore, is an essential safety tool when riding with anyone else. Discussing the rules, expectations, and methods of riding together beforehand will prevent misunderstandings—or worse—when out on the road. Communication extends to being able to let the group know when you need a pit stop, if you're in urgent need of a snack, or if something feels off with your bike. If you have Bluetooth devices, are you able to sync them before you leave so you can talk as needed while riding? Do you use common hand signals? Motorcyclists typically use a universal set of signs, but my husband and I know American Sign Language and often use it when riding. A friend and her husband SCUBA dive together, and they use another set of signs. Riding with my friend means that we need to agree on which signs mean what because we could potentially be "speaking" in one of three completely different languages.

Communication should also extend to debriefing after a ride to allow the group to talk about anything unexpected that happened and how it was handled, thus creating a potential teachable moment about how to ride together. While not all groups do this, it can add to the safety of your group outings in the future.

Breaking into smaller groups is a wise option when the numbers become too large. A leader can usually manage watching out for four to five riders, but after that, it's too hard to keep an eye on everyone as the bikes stretch out. When some riders go slower and others want to speed up, the chances of losing someone increase. Sometimes groups are divided into smaller groups by ability level or pace and other times simply due to size. Either way, this reduces the risk of accidents, makes it easier to get through stop signs and stop lights, and can help new riders get to know others more easily when the group stops for breaks.

A Polite Escape

A ride leader shared one of her favorite tips for politely escaping a group ride without tipping your hand: the imaginary urgent text message or phone call. "A call came in while we were riding, and I just noticed the voicemail." Taking a moment to pretend to listen to it, you realize that a sudden "change of plans" necessitates your immediate return home. "I'm so sorry, and I hate to leave everyone when I'm having such a great time, but my family needs me at home right away." In this case, knowing your route and how to get yourself back is important: make sure that you can get home safely and that you are able to contact help should anything go awry once you leave the group.

As with a solo ride, you should always have an escape plan when riding with a group. In this case, the escape plan refers to being able to leave the group if, for any reason, it doesn't feel right to you or takes you out of your comfort zone. A pre-ride discussion online with a welcoming group of women riders chatting about the upcoming leisurely day trip may, in real life, turn out to be a pack of racing demons flying around tight turns and ignoring posted speed signs. The women may appear friendly and open at the start of the day and become cliquey and rude by lunchtime. The slow crawl of a group, frequent stops for gas, and demand that you all stay in strict formation may stifle your ability to set your own pace. Or there may be no obvious issues; you may simply realize that riding with others isn't for you after giving it a whirl. Also as with riding solo, a GPS, cell phone, and satellite tracking device are important safety tools to have with you at all times, especially if you aren't sure where you are going, don't know the roads well, and are riding with a new group.

Adding a Passenger

Before I went on my first ride with my husband, he explained everything I would need to know for us to be safe, not only for myself as a passenger but also for him as the driver. He taught me how he wanted me to get on and off the bike and asked me to keep my feet on the foot pegs when we stopped (instead of putting them down on the road). He instructed me to be "invisible," meaning to let the bike dictate what my body did and to not "help" him in any way. This was in contrast to what I had heard from others years before about leaning into the turns, but my job was to do what he wanted because he was the one driving. We didn't have a communication system at that time, so he told me how to let him know if I needed anything. Education completed, I hopped on the back and off we went. I quickly learned that he was correct: my body, if relaxed and comfortable, naturally leaned into the turns; I didn't have to do anything except enjoy the ride.

What I also learned was how much more work my husband had to do with me on the back. The bike was heavier and took longer to stop, and he could feel every shift I made on my seat. Those shifts often caused slight changes in the bike's center of gravity and affected its handling. It was important that I let him know when I needed to move and what I was doing so he could adjust accordingly. When we came to stops, I sat perfectly still so as not to add to the challenge of holding up the bike. When I began riding on my own, I realized even further how much any added weight affected the motorcycle's handling and that it was important to take some time to get used to the difference.

Before taking someone for a ride, make sure you understand how it will affect your riding and that you are comfortable with the added weight and responsibility. Review your expectations with your passenger and have a way to communicate while in motion. Maintain a similar concern for your passenger's safety and protective gear as you do for yourself. The responsibility for getting where you are going lies with you; make it clear that you, as the driver, are in charge. If you aren't comfortable carrying a passenger, be sure to assert yourself; there isn't room on the bike for being nice.

Breakdowns

Even a perfectly maintained motorcycle can have a bad day, and that bad day usually happens at an inopportune place or time. Life would be so much easier if breakdowns occurred in the comfort of your garage or in the parking lot of your mechanic's shop, but, alas, it rarely happens that way. You've been a diligent owner: you've recently had

Make sure that passing traffic can easily see you if you are on the side of the road.

A broken turn signal will not affect how the bike runs but could affect your safety.

your bike in for routine maintenance and, before a trip, you check your oil, pull out your pressure gauge to make sure that your tires are just right, and confirm that the gas tank is full. As you're packing up for your long weekend ride, you're thinking, "I've covered everything. What could possibly go wrong?"

And for the first many miles, nothing does. It's only when you've turned down the gorgeous two-lane road that winds along the gently flowing river on the way to your campground that you notice your bike is handling differently. The handlebars are more wobbly than normal, and something just feels wrong. You need to stop and figure out what's happening.

The first rule of any breakdown is to get off the road safely. What determines "safe" will depend on where you are riding. If on an interstate, is there an off ramp coming up so you can exit and find a quiet street or parking lot? If not, can you pull to the right side of the freeway and look for the widest area of shoulder to give you the largest margin between you and the traffic whizzing by? No matter the size of the road you are on, are you easily visible to motorists approaching from either direction? Are you in a well-lit spot? Are you on a safe surface, or are you surrounded by a lot of gravel, potholes, or an uneven camber where you might drop your bike and complicate matters further?

A state patrolman, who is also a motorcyclist, shared with me that the side of the road is one of the most dangerous places to stop, putting you at risk of being hit by an inattentive driver or one who becomes fixated on whatever that object is (you) on the shoulder and inadvertently aims right for it. Remember, we go where we look, even in a car. Being in a large group can give you a false sense of security; it won't protect you or your friends from an automobile barreling down the highway at high speed. Anything that gets you as far as possible from a potentially far worse situation than a broken-down bike is your first priority.

Most motorcyclists, seeing another bike parked alongside the road, will slow down or stop to see if they can render assistance. If you see a bike approaching and don't need help, a quick thumbs-up and a wave will let the rider know that you are OK. Placing your helmet on the ground behind your bike is typically understood as a sign that you do need help. We once came upon a rider on the side of a busy road who, as we neared, made the universal sign for telephone. My husband and I initially interpreted this signal differently: was he asking us to call someone or telling us that he had already made the call? We circled back around and pulled in behind him to make sure that he was OK. As it turned out, he had been sitting there for more than four hours in the heat, without water, and without a single person stopping to help. He was hot, dehydrated, and miserable. He told us that he had run out of gas, but with the nearest station several miles away, he hadn't felt safe leaving his bike. We gave him one of our spare water bottles to first quench his thirst and then serve as a container, and we used some extra tubing from our hydration system to fashion a gas can. We were able to siphon enough fuel out of our tank to get him into town, and we followed him until we knew he had safely made it and could refill his tank. While running out of gas shouldn't, but can, happen to anyone, this motorcyclist didn't know how to let others know he needed help. In addition, he wasn't prepared for the length of time he had to sit by the side of the road, nor was he prepared for the lack of shade on what was a very hot, sunny day.

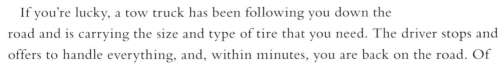

Let's return to the wobbly motorcycle scenario. Knowing that you need to find a safe place to stop, you ride for a few more miles until you notice an old deserted gas station with a weed-filled but manageable parking area just ahead. A quick assessment reassures you that you can safely navigate the terrain, and your hand signal alerts your riding buddies that you're turning in so they can follow you. Putting the sidestand down, you get off the bike to see what's going on. It takes a few minutes and a lot of looking until you spot the culprit: a screw embedded in your tire, causing a slow leak. After a deep sigh of relief that the tire wasn't catastrophically damaged when it hit the screw, you plop down on a chunk of concrete wall left over from the station's better days to contemplate what to do.

If you're lucky, a tow truck has been following you down the road and is carrying the size and type of tire that you need. The driver stops and offers to handle everything, and, within minutes, you are back on the road. Of

course, the odds of such an occurrence are far less likely than getting the screw in your tire in the first place, and if it should ever happen, be sure to pick up a lottery ticket once you are back in town. Realistically, you will need to have roadside assistance programmed into your phone, good cell coverage in your remote location, and plenty of patience to twiddle your thumbs while you wait for someone to show up—or, a much better option: the knowledge of how to repair your own tire.

There are many situations that require a rider to wait for a tow truck when what is wrong with the bike is beyond the ability of the best mechanic to fix on the side of the road. For these types of breakdowns, it's wise to belong to a roadside assistance program such as those offered through some manufacturers, riding clubs, or AAA. But there are numerous minor breakdowns that the average rider can handle with a bit of common sense, the right tools, and some basic training in what to do. The key is to make sure you that have all three every time you leave home on your bike.

"You will never suffer a punctured tire until you leave the repair kit at home."

—Murphy's Law for Motorcycles #7

Common sense is hard to teach but important to have with you if you need to deal with an unplanned roadside repair. Knowing where things are on your bike, being able to evaluate what is going on and what the symptoms may be telling you, and working methodically can save you time and effort and may even prevent further damage. Being aware of the resources available to you can increase the potential for solving problems, and thinking things through before diving in may give you a chance to come up with some creative solutions that will at least get you back to civilization and the repair shop.

Two hundred miles into my first SaddleSore (a 1,000-mile ride in twenty-four hours), we were parked for lunch when a teenager on a Sting-Ray bicycle split between our bike and its neighbor, hitting ours and knocking it over onto the footpeg of our friend's. The most noticeable damage was to the windscreen: a third of it had been broken off. Continuing on without some kind of repair would leave what remained to flap in its absence, not to mention the impact that the wind would have on my husband once we got the bike back up to speed. After a quick brainstorming session among all the riders, we pulled the duct tape from our toolkit. We had soon securely swathed the screen in the familiar gray, and because most riders don't look through—but instead over—the windscreen, our solution was brilliant, cheap, and workable. We did not have to abort the SaddleSore, and we were able to quickly stow our tools and get back on our way.

Most new motorcycles come with a very basic tool kit and a minimalist troubleshooting guide in the owner's manual. Before going for your first few rides, take the time to explore what's in your kit and figure out what might be helpful to supplement the meager ration of supplies. A small roll of duct tape and a handful of zip ties can be used for a multitude of repairs, and a flashlight for seeing into tiny crevices and tight spaces is invaluable. Carry a tire-repair kit that includes compressed air, and keep a zipper-seal plastic bag with spare bulbs and fuses always with you. A good multipurpose knife or Leatherman will always come in handy, and an adjustable wrench, a pair of pliers, an Allen wrench, and both Phillips and flathead screwdrivers should round out your basic kit. While it's best if you can patch a tire or reattach a loose wire yourself, simply having these tools may help someone who stops to assist you in case you can't get yourself back on the road.

Now that you have stocked your bike with the essentials needed in case of a breakdown, do you know how to use them? Plugging a tire takes a

bit of practice, and you should know how to locate fuses and access your lightbulbs in case you need to replace them. Taking an introductory class in motorcycle repairs will expose you to some of the common skills that may come in handy later on, as will spending time with a knowledgeable friend or your mechanic. You don't need to become a wrench; you simply need to know enough to get yourself going again.

Preparing for Weather

If you only ride on sunny Sundays when there is a zero chance of a sudden afternoon thunderstorm or unexpected wind gusts, your primary safety consideration may be how much sunscreen to put on. But if you head off in favorable conditions with the understanding that it can all change in an instant, carrying the right gear is essential.

I live in the Pacific Northwest, and rain is a given here. If I want to ride, I need to be prepared to get wet. I've learned to slow down and give myself more time when the roads are slick and to permit more space between others on the road and me to allow for increased reaction times. Despite the frequency of precipitation around here, the automobile drivers apparently forget how to drive as soon as the first raindrop appears, and I want to be prepared for anything that they may throw my way. Sudden lane changes, irrationally slow speeds, and jerky stops are among the reactions that I expect and plan for.

Knowing the typical weather patterns in your area and how they affect drivers of all skill levels will help you be mentally prepared to navigate the conditions as they occur. No matter what type of weather you encounter—whether rain, wind, sleet, or even snow—slowing down will often mean a better ride and a safe return home.

Riding when soaked can cause chills, and if you get too cold, you may not be safe to continue on the road. If your outer gear isn't already waterproof, have a rain suit and a pair of gloves with you at all times that can keep you warm and dry. Be sure to find a safe place to stop and put on your waterproof layer; remember, putting it on before you get wet will provide the maximum protection. I also carry a dual-purpose hat that is waterproof and can provide sun protection should I need to get off my bike and remove my helmet for any reason. It has definitely come in handy when I've had to fix something on my bike in 100-degree weather without a spot of shade for miles.

Similarly, if you are riding in extreme heat, having a way to consume fluids can mean the difference between simply being uncomfortable and becoming dizzy and disoriented from dehydration. Some riders add water bladders or coolers to their bikes, using a hose with a bite valve to deliver the liquid while driving. Others wear small backpacks with hydration systems, the same kind that hikers use when out in the woods. Carrying spare water bottles in a top box or saddlebag will tide you over in between stops at mini-marts or gas stations should you need to take a break along the road.

If you need glasses to drive, bring a spare pair.

The same weather that you can handle by day may be more challenging when it's dark. Becoming comfortable with night riding before adding the complications of rain, wind, or cold should be your first strategy. If you plan to ride at all times of day or night, make sure that your bike has adequate lighting and that you have adequate protection from the elements. It's even colder when the sun goes down, and it's often harder to maintain focus and a positive attitude when you can't see as far into the distance. Some riders have vision problems that affect their ability to ride at night.

Medical or Physical Concerns

Kate Johnston, who set the Iron Butt Association's woman's record for riding from Key West, Florida, to Prudhoe Bay, Alaska, and back again in twenty-four days is a type I diabetic, as was her mentor and role model, John Ryan. Bob Mutchler, whose story I tell in my book From *Iron Lung to Iron Butt: Riding Polio into History*, has walked with crutches and braces from the effects of polio as an infant, yet he has competed in five Iron Butt rallies. There are numerous stories of riders with physical or medical challenges who have fully embraced motorcycling and are extremely successful. Each has found a way to adapt or modify his or her bike or riding style to find whatever works. Kate learned the hard way that her normal ability to listen to her body when off the bike wasn't as sharp while riding and that the demands of endurance riding required a different level of attention. She created a routine for checking her glucose levels at every stop, far more often than when in a car or at home. She ate more frequently, carried ample supplies, and had a Spot tracker for emergencies. Bob rides with a sidecar and an adapted hand shifter; when his sidecar malfunctioned and his brakes failed on a twisty mountain road, and he knew that he was going to crash, he was mentally prepared and kept his head. He was wearing all of the protective gear, and he steered the rig as best he could, giving him the best chance for minimizing injuries, which he was able to accomplish.

If you wear contacts or glasses, do you carry spares? I had the habit of taking off my glasses while putting on my helmet, only to drive off with them still on the rear seat. To prevent that from recurring, I mounted a tiny ring in a visible location on the handlebars where I hang my glasses when I take them off and can see them if I forget to put them back on. My husband wears hearing aids, which he

I was paying too much attention to the cars behind me; one kept creeping up too close and then would back off. I wasn't watching the road in front of me as carefully as I needed to, and I came into a corner too fast. I was only going about 15 mph, but it was a tight turn, and I missed it. I high-sided the bike and landed in the ditch beside the road. I was lucky; I was banged up, but nothing was broken except parts of my bike. A guy on a Harley stopped to help me get it back up, and I was able to call someone to bring a trailer to get it back home. Two things I learned: to keep my focus primarily on the road ahead and that I loved working on bikes. I'm now in school to become a motorcycle mechanic.

Accidents can have physical and emotional impacts on everyone involved.

has to remove when riding. He has a routine and, when riding, he always places the case in the same location in his saddlebag, near his gloves.

Whatever issues you may be dealing with, explore the necessary adaptations and routines to make riding not only a positive experience but also a safe one. Hearing aids and glasses are expensive to replace; too high or too low blood sugar can lead to a serious accident. Take the time to figure it out, and remember that whatever works for you in a car may not work the same on a bike.

In Case of Accident...

Preparing for most scenarios while riding means being prepared for the misfortune of being involved in an accident, whether as a victim, a first responder, or a witness. Doing everything to avoid an accident is, of course, the wisest choice, but life happens and sometimes that means an accident. In the first moments of stunned disbelief following a crash, it may be hard to remember what to do, but having a plan ahead of time may save you unnecessary heartaches later.

There are courses available on accident-scene management or motorcycle crash-scene safety that will provide invaluable information and training for both the victim and the bystanders. Knowing what to do, what not to do, and how to communicate with medical personnel can save lives, alleviate suffering, and help get the victims on the road to recovery more quickly. These courses provide instruction on how to assess the situation and injuries, how to administer

basic first aid, how to safely remove helmets or gear, and how to work with the EMS teams effectively. Accident Scene Management (http://roadguardians.org) is among several organizations that teach these courses.

Accidents happen quickly and unexpectedly. In the first few moments, it can be difficult, if not impossible, to comprehend what occurred. At the same time, people are asking questions, dealing with injuries, and wanting statements. As a bystander, securing the scene to protect victims and prevent further injuries is your first priority, and providing first aid to anyone injured until EMS comes is of vital importance. Once trained professionals have arrived, you can help by taking a variety of pictures of the motorcycle and any other vehicles before they are moved and getting witness statements; these measures can assist the victim in dealing with police and insurance as well as with understanding what happened for their own healing and learning. Small details may have large impacts later on, and the more information the victims have available to them, the better.

If you are the victim, you may be in shock, particularly if you sustained any injuries, so it is best to follow the advice of most insurance companies and say as little as possible: do not admit fault until you truly understand what has happened. Those conversations can take place at a later time, when you have recovered from the initial insult to your body and bike and are able to think clearly.

I carry laminated cards with personal information with me at all times. I have one in my wallet and another in the top pocket of my riding jacket. They include emergency contacts, my blood type, a list of medications I take regularly, the name and phone number of my personal physician, and my insurance information. Some riders carry this information in specially designed holders with bright labels mounted on their helmets or jackets. In the event of an accident, if you are unable to speak for yourself, these cards will be your voice. Medical personnel not only will be able to quickly access your medical history but also will be able to notify whomever you have designated in your contacts.

I also have evacuation insurance. In my case, when I was injured and unable to ride my bike back to the West Coast following an accident in the East, they transported the bike home without any hassles or surcharges. The money I saved more than compensated for the two-year premium I had paid. Carry your insurance cards with you at all times on the bike and make sure your premiums are up to date.

Getting back on the bike following any type of accident may evoke fear and anxiety. Being safe means being able to focus on the task at hand. It's perfectly normal to have some trepidation when you first head out, but if you find yourself reliving your experience or if you feel jumpy and overly watchful, you may want to consider getting help with the leftover effects from your accident. Psychotherapy to address the trauma, mental-skills coaching to help you bring your attention back to riding, or a refresher course to rebuild your confidence on the bike may be of help. Look for someone who understands and supports your desire to ride again but who also allows you the space to figure out if motorcycling is still right for you.

Making the effort to think through your riding habits, and planning for and rehearsing situations that might arise, will help reduce your risks when out on the road. Safety is an all-encompassing topic: learning to ride well, taking reasonable and proven safety measures, knowing the people you are riding with, being prepared for emergencies whether alone or in a group, and listening to your gut are all within your control and are part of your responsibility as a rider. Should an accident happen, taking the time to fully recover both physically and mentally is essential for returning to the sport. Having fun on the motorcycle is great; coming home safely at the end of the day is even better.

~When I first got my license, I went out to practice my skills and noticed a really hot guy, shirtless, in a convertible pulling up next to me. He was smiling at me, and I couldn't keep from glancing over at him, smiling back inside my helmet. I was so caught up with our little flirtation that I failed to notice that his lane was an exit only, and he was turning off to the right. I glanced ahead just in time to see the light in my lane changing to red. Frantically grabbing my brakes, I screeched and slid into the lane on my left, coming to a halt just in front of a woman in a minivan. Luckily, she had seen me and braked in time to avoid a collision. I learned a valuable lesson that day: save the flirting for off the motorcycle! Later, I was sharing my story while waiting for my bike to be serviced, and a guy sitting nearby with a cast on his leg started laughing. He'd been doing the same thing—flirting with a woman on a bike—and when they both came to a stop, he was so focused on her that he completely forgot to put his feet down. He tipped over and the motorcycle caught his leg underneath, breaking his ankle. Looking at his crutches and the size of his cast, I was glad I escaped with only my pride damaged.~

Chapter 8

Putting It All Together

The freedom of riding solo can be empowering.

You've dutifully taken your instructional courses, had fun shopping for your perfect bike and protective gear, spent hours practicing your U-turns and quick stops—what to do next? Before jumping into anything too quickly, take some time to reflect on the type of motorcyclist you are, what you love about riding and what isn't your cup of tea, and how you envision your riding in the future. Do you prefer going out alone or with others? Do you want to hang out with a group of folks who share your obsession with a particular brand of bike, or are you more of the eclectic type, intrigued by the mix of whoever shows up on whatever to go for a ride together? Do you find yourself leafing through *Backroads* magazine, sighing over the descriptions of weekend getaways through tiny towns and quaint country inns? Have you accompanied a girlfriend on a brief off-road shortcut only to discover a previously unknown passion for adventure riding? When you've watched some of your friends flying around the track, did the thought of zipping through turns at high speed get your adrenaline pumping as well? Can you imagine taking off from work on a Friday to ride hundreds of miles across the country merely to join friends for a barbecue lunch and some tire kicking before hopping back on the bike to be home in time for work again on Monday morning? Or is it possible you're an everywoman, wanting to pack your camping gear on the bike one weekend for an outing with your riding group, commute to work during the week, join your local club for a poker run the next Saturday, and then take a solo ride through the countryside to clear your head on Sunday, all while perusing the Internet to figure out which touring company to choose for your next adventure vacation? There's no need to confine your riding to a single style: whatever resonates with you is where you should be riding, and wherever you are riding, there's a community to support your passion.

Riding Solo

Groups are great, and having the support of other riders, whether female or male, can be very encouraging, especially for newer riders. But no matter your ultimate goal for your motorcycling, there is much to be gained by riding alone at least some of the time. If you always ride with someone else, you will miss the opportunity to push your personal envelope and confront issues you'd otherwise not get the chance to solve by yourself. One of the common themes I hear from women riders is the feeling of competence that comes from mastering their bikes, particularly the nuances of their mechanical operation, an area where they usually don't spend much time or energy outside of motorcycling. The experience of empowerment comes from doing, not thinking about or watching someone else doing.

My earliest riding experiences were all with my husband, two-up and always together, whether solving problems during a rally or figuring out how to navigate an unknown city during rush hour. However, he made all the technical decisions, such as where it was safest to park the bike or how to fix any mechanical problems. I might have shared my input, but it was just as likely that I tuned out and let him take care of the pesky details. We really didn't need two brains for that: he was the

driver, he had the knowledge and the interest, and it naturally made sense for him to figure it out. I was the navigator and was focused on my role of planning routes and finding the best roads. Our routines changed only slightly when I started riding my own bike because I was still out with him. It wasn't until I began taking off alone that I felt the impact of having to deal with whatever I was confronted with instead of deferring to a more

Being a solo rider means that you're the only problem-solver and navigator, but it can bring great excitement over your achievements.

experienced rider. If I wasn't interested in minor details, too bad! They needed attending, and I was the only one there to do the attending.

The more I rode alone, the more I liked the feeling of having to figure things out. Even the simplest challenge of where to make a U-turn when I drove past the driveway I was looking for became a test of my ability to sort out the road conditions, the traffic, and my anxieties about falling if I screwed up. No one was offering an opinion, sharing their sage advice, or leading the way. If I fell, I'd have to face the embarrassment alone, and I'd have to get the bike back up off the ground either by myself or by asking a stranger for help. Pulling into a gas station meant that I was the one who had to wrestle the pump into the narrow opening on my bike rather than running into the mini-mart to purchase my Frappuccino while my husband did all of the work. The tiniest details were now up to me, and, in the same way that I was building my riding skills, I was building my confidence in my problem-solving skills.

My experience parallels those of many of the women I've met in a wide variety of motorcycling circles. It doesn't matter how long they've been riding—what we all have in common is that something changed when we started. And for me and every other woman, it changed exponentially when we ventured off alone. Some of the gals I listened to spoke of learning alone; there weren't any other riders, let alone women riders, to go out with. If they wanted to ride, they had no choice but to get on the bike and figure it out. Their confidence was evident; they weren't afraid to go anywhere or handle anything because they'd already faced some of their greatest fears and challenges.

There is no need to put pressure on yourself or have any expectations about riding alone; it is merely an opportunity to explore an area of riding that you may not yet have tapped and to find out how you feel about it. Even short solo trips to the store will stir up unexpected reactions if you've always traveled with someone else. Whether it's a sense of fear or a sudden rush of freedom, experiencing these emotions can help you continue your growth toward being a well-rounded, skilled motorcyclist. If you feel fear, is there a skill that you still need to learn that might help you feel more comfortable? If you feel a thrill, is it possible that you've been stuck in your comfort zone and it's time to stretch your wings a bit more? No matter what you decide, if you choose to ride solo, it's important that you are ready to take care of yourself and your bike.

The Author's Experiences

I'm a very independent person: I've traveled around the world solo, and I love spending an entertaining meal alone, people-watching in a crowded diner or finding a quiet corner to sit and read a good book. I frequently become overwhelmed in large groups, and I definitely need a lot of downtime to recharge. I routinely tackle complex problems without help from others and often prefer working on projects alone. My parents were interior designers; they hired out the technical details of furniture installation and wiring, so mechanics and machines were not part of my upbringing, and growing that part of my skill set hadn't been on my bucket list. It wasn't until I started riding without my partner, a friend, or in a group that I had to confront both my lack of interest and my even greater lack of skills. Once I did, however, I found that I could figure out solutions to many problems myself. I now take pride in my ability to communicate with other riders about my bike, and, although I prefer heading out with my husband or girlfriends for most rides, I definitely enjoy riding places by myself and knowing that I can take care of most issues that may arise.

Driver or Pillion?

My first significant experiences as a motorcyclist were on the back, or pillion, seat. The riding community I was fortunate to become a part of was very welcoming to passengers. There was no derisive language about the "bitch seat" and no feelings that I was any less of a rider because I wasn't holding the handlebars. I didn't experience any comments that women belonged in the back; that would not have gone over well with me. In some motorcycling cultures, the term "riding bitch" may be acceptable and even preferred, but in others, it can be seen as a

When riding by
yourself, you can
truly do your own
thing.

diminishment of the passenger, a sense that you are somehow "less than" if you aren't a driver. Having completed two eleven-day Iron Butt Rallies as a pillion, I believe my role was just as challenging and important as that of my husband, who was in the front seat. My belief, and that of my riding community, is that no matter where you are riding, you are a motorcyclist.

Remaining on the passenger seat should be considered a well-thought-out choice to spend time with your partner, enjoying the scenery and the relaxation, or a decision that driving isn't right for you. Riding pillion is still a commitment to being together, sharing a passion for riding. For some riders, it may be a practical consideration due to medical or financial constraints. Being unable to see at night or the costs of purchasing and maintaining two bikes are only two of many reasons for opting to share one motorcycle. It may be a temporary choice, such as touring Europe two-up instead of each riding your own bike like you do at home. As pillion, one of you can become the navigator, dealing with incomprehensible names on narrow lanes, freeing your partner to focus on avoiding wrong turns and collisions with foreign drivers familiar with the twists and turns of their local roads. And,

We realized that if we each rode on our own, we could take longer trips and carry more. Our camping gear would finally fit without thinking about towing a trailer!

of course, someone has to take the amazing photographs that can only be captured while in motion.

Some of you will, like I did, make the decision to move from pillion to driver. The first time I tried it was in response to internal pressure that I should be on my own. Intellectually, I knew I was more than capable of learning how to manage a bike, and even taking the class was fun. What I was ignoring was that I wasn't ready emotionally. There was too much going on elsewhere in our lives, and the timing wasn't right. I wasn't sufficiently committed or focused to devote the time and energy to improving my skills, and I wasn't internally motivated to be riding solo. Remaining on the pillion seat was a well-considered, wise choice for me at that point in my motorcycling journey. When I finally did make the move to my own bike, it was entirely driven by my personal desire to do so, and I have loved every minute of the transition. I knew I had nothing to prove and no one to answer to, and I felt a yearning inside of me to get out and ride. I have no regrets about my time riding pillion; I learned far more than I ever imagined in those years, and both my relationship and I grew immensely from navigating the complexities of sharing a single bike with my husband. My experiences as a passenger have made me the rider and the person I am today.

The author's book Two-Up *draws heavily from her experiences riding pillion with her husband.*

Whichever seat you choose, it needs to be the one that's right one for you, no one else. At any time you so desire, give yourself permission to change your mind. There is no right way to ride, only the right way for you. Whatever your decision, connecting with others and building your riding community can be one of the best parts of motorcycling.

Types of Riding

Just as there are numerous brands and models of motorcycles, there are a wide variety of ways to ride them. Many riders start with a single style of riding, such as street, off-road, or sport, but soon venture off into other areas. Sometimes these moves are evolutionary, such as learning on the street and then discovering off-road and never looking back, while often they are additive, such as getting a dual-sport bike once you discover that you like both on- and off-road riding. I currently own two bikes, one for the street and one for the dirt, and I'm debating

I don't feel a need to explain to anyone why I have several motorcycles. Those who ride get it, and those who don't, never will.

which bike will be next on my shopping list because I want to continue long-distance riding (comfort, weight, and weather protection), go down forestry roads to find remote campsites (medium-weight dirt or dual-sport bike), and maybe be able to head out for a women's track day (lighter weight sport bike). As many enthusiasts say, you can never have too many motorcycles, although my budget may tell me otherwise. While most riders attempt to find a single motorcycle to meet most of their requirements, understanding the different options for getting out on a bike may open new opportunities for you to expand your riding experiences.

Adventure riding is a self-defined category that essentially covers any type of

A long-distance rider starts the first leg of the Iron Butt Rally.

motorcycling that seems adventurous to you, the person who is participating in it. Typically, it refers to heading out and facing whatever challenges there are to be confronted, and often that includes both on- and off-road rides. World travel, paved roads in remote locales, dirt ruts off the beaten track, river crossings—anything that gets the rider out and away from her routine commute to work. Bikes in this category attempt to bridge the gap between touring and dirt, giving up some features of one in order to be prepared to accomplish the tasks of the other. It's one of the fastest growing segments in the industry as more and more riders discover the joys of seeking out new challenges, and manufacturers are rushing to introduce new models every year to meet the demand.

Touring refers to the use of a motorcycle as a means of travel, whether around your local region or across the entire globe. Touring riders tend to savor the journey, stopping to smell the flowers and take in the sights. Some camp, while others stay in hotels or with friends; the commonality is found in spending time on their bikes, soaking up the environment and the people they meet along the way. Touring bikes are designed to carry a lot of gear and offer greater protection from the elements. Both touring and adventure riders can find companies catering to these markets throughout the world, providing motorcycle rentals and guided tours for those wishing to combine a fun vacation with an exhilarating ride.

Long-distance riders love to pound out the miles, piling up 800- to 1,000-mile days without blinking an eye. Many complete documented rides, such as the previously mentioned SaddleSore 1,000 or a 50 CC Quest, riding between the Pacific Coast and the Atlantic Coast in either direction in fifty hours or less, all for recognition from the Iron Butt Association. In addition, there are numerous rallies, or scavenger hunts, which combine long distances with bonuses. These bonuses can be unique or unusual locations, landmarks, or oddities, and they often send riders down roads known for great riding. Rallies can vary from one to several days in duration up to the highly regarded Iron Butt Rally, which takes place over eleven days. Some rallies are quite competitive, whereas some lean more toward a good excuse to go for a ride and meet up with friends for a banquet at the finish, but even the competitive rallies welcome newcomers who are excited to learn more about the sport.

Off-road, or dirt, riding encompasses a wide range of venues, including simply taking off on local Forest Service roads or creating a course in your own backyard. Many riders take dirt-riding classes simply to improve their overall motorcycling skills and to prepare for those moments when they encounter the unexpected road construction or long gravel driveway. But there are those for whom the chance to explore where the path will take them, camping in remote locations accessible only by bike and navigating and dodging whatever obstacles are in their way, becomes their passion. Getting dirty, muddy, and wet are part of the fun, and falling down is a given. Kids as young as six can learn to ride on dirt, and many families enjoy sharing the experience of off-roading together.

There are numerous competitive events for those drawn to dirt, grit, and mud. Motocross refers to races that take place on a combination of natural

Adventure can happen wherever the road takes you.

The Women's Guide to Motorcycling

Races are held on tracks as well as on natural terrain.

and man-made courses. These races are tests of agility and speed over jumps, hills, berms, washboards, and tight turns. Up to forty riders at a time may start, and the winner is the first to finish the course or the first to complete the required number of laps. Freestyle motocross adds judging the acrobatic quality of the jumps into the mix. As the popularity of motocross continues to grow, numerous other events have been added to the menu, including supermoto, which combines on- and off-road sections, and vintage, which limits bikes to models predating 1975.

Trials take place on dirt courses, and the riders are expected to navigate the obstacles without putting their feet down. Time and observation trials add a time element to the contest. Trial courses can be indoors, in stadiums, or in natural settings. Hillclimbing is just like it sounds: climbing extremely steep hills on a motorcycle. Riders compete solo against the clock or head-to-head with another rider. Many of the hills are so steep that simply completing the course is a challenge. In that case, the rider who makes it the greatest distance will take the prize.

Enduro races take place over natural terrain, mixing challenging "test" sections with easier trails or fire roads. These events are timed, and riders go from checkpoint to checkpoint, following specific guidelines and directions. Some riders enjoy competing in dirt track races. These are held on half-mile and mile tracks; some, called TT races, include tight turns and a jump. Hare scrambles are off-road events in which all of the riders start at once and navigate marked looped courses through open fields, forests, or deserts. The winner is either the first one to complete a set number of laps or, typically, the one in the lead at the two-hour time limit.

Track days are becoming fairly common across the country, offering everyday riders the chance to learn and practice on closed-circuit paved courses. Some of these include instruction, and some are open to all levels and styles of bike. Track days can be a great way to experiment with speed in a safe environment to see if it's something that you want to pursue further. Track days can also help improve a rider's overall riding skills, especially cornering, even if she never intends to race.

If you find yourself falling in love with speed, training for the track is only one of many directions open to you. Road racing takes place on public roads that have been closed specifically for the event. The American Motorcycle Association, for example, sponsors the Road Race Grand Championships, which are open to club-level riders, in Ohio every summer. Landspeed racing pits the rider against the clock on a 1- to 3-mile perfectly level and straight course at a location such as the Bonneville Salt Flats. Speedway racing uses an oval dirt or shale track but limits the bike to one gear and no brakes, challenging the rider's ability to manage the bike while competing head-to-head with other racers over a very short course of a quarter mile or less. Endurance racing is designed for teams to compete over a set distance or covering as many laps as possible within a set length of time, such as twenty-four hours. Teams can change drivers during the event as needed.

Sidecar racing encompasses both traditionally styled sidecars competing against similar models as well as modern, specially designed motorcycles with custom-built sidecars. Riders and passengers work together to maximize performance, with the passenger often seen hanging over the road in turns. For those who live in cold winter climates, ice racing can be a great challenge. Races take place on ice tracks, and tires are fitted with metal spikes or screws.

Doing Your Research

Numerous websites give their picks for the top-ten motorcycle rides, best motorcycle roads, and best motorcycle trips in the United States. If you're looking for places to ride, you'll more than likely be overwhelmed by the choices and at the same time excited to get out and explore. Planning trips, whether across town on yet-to-be-discovered back roads or across the country, becomes an adventure in itself with some of these sites. Examples include OpenRoadJourney (www.openroadjourney.com), Harley-Davidson Ride Planner (www.harley-davidson.com, under "Owners" tab), Sunday Morning Rides (www.sundaymorningrides.com), and Best Biking Roads (www.bestbikingroads.com). These are just a few examples, and you may also find websites tailored to your specific area.

The beauty of motorcycling is that you aren't forced into a single choice. Yes, the bike you purchase may limit some of your options, but whenever you want to explore a new path, you can always borrow, rent, or even purchase a new or used motorcycle to see if it's for you. You'll be able to find plenty of support and guidance along the way from others whose passion is sharing their love of riding and experience with you. Remember, you can always get a bigger garage.

Where to Ride: Finding Great Roads

Whenever I am in a new part of the country, I want to explore all the places where locals like to ride. They typically know the great roads, but how do I gain their knowledge as a newcomer? How do you learn where to ride when you're first starting out? Even in familiar territory, how do you discover new places? I love spending time on the computer, poring over maps, trying to figure out how to get somewhere I've been numerous times before but on roads I've never taken. Sometimes, in the process, I discover a new favorite.

Books like *Destination Highways* and magazines such as *Backroads* offer motorcyclists detailed routes and maps to follow, sharing secrets known to those familiar with an area with the greater riding public. Keeping a file of potential trips I'd like to take if I'm ever in an area mentioned in an article triggers my memory when the time arrives and I'm looking for a few good roads. I use the Internet when I will be in a yet-to-be explored place, searching by entering "motorcycle roads in *xyz* state," and have found great success with that method. Websites often include rider reviews and little details that not only help me plan an interesting route but also take into account the best places to eat, interesting hotels, or scenic spots where I can get off the bike for a short rest.

Online forums are also great places to do your research. If you post questions that detail what you are looking for, how far you want to ride, the type of riding

you like to do, and the things you would like to do along the way, you will usually get a plethora of opinions and ideas from people who have actually traveled the roads. Checking state transportation websites will help you find road construction or road closure notices, which can come in handy if you don't want to get stuck in traffic or have to ride miles out of your way following detour signs. Post your own reviews of roads and routes after you spend time riding them. Sharing your insights and opinions can help others plan their trips, just as someone offered their wisdom to you.

With almost everyone using smartphones, it's not surprising to find motorcycling apps on most platforms. You can use apps to find great roads, learn of approaching weather systems, plan for traffic, find useful first-aid information, and even watch simple mechanical demonstrations for minor repairs. Having all of this technology at your fingertips will allow you to modify your route while on the road, whether to take advantage of a previously unknown road or navigate around an approaching storm or traffic bottleneck. Some apps let you share your route with friends in real time so they can meet up with you along the way.

Finally, ask your riding friends to take you out and show you some of their favorite routes. I've often been surprised at the incredibly fun roads in my own backyard that I never would have known about if not for spending time with other riders who let me tag along while they share their knowledge with me.

Chapter 9

Getting Involved

Joining a Group

Those who love groups, and especially all-female groups, do so with a passion. Their eyes light up when they talk about sharing their excitement for riding with others who not only "get it" but who participate in it fully as well. Watching these women gush over each other's bikes or share information about how to handle a repair while laughing about their latest dating woes evokes a strong desire to be part of the camaraderie. It truly becomes a family for many, and the connections often extend far beyond riding. These women form deep bonds and willingly support each other in times of joy as well as times of need.

I look forward to riding with my group. We go out once a week and check out different roads in the area. We're mostly on sport bikes, but <u>anyone</u> is welcome as long as they're female and on two wheels. Gay, straight, married, single, <u>old, young</u>; it doesn't matter, as long as they want to ride. I love being badass with my girls, cruising. I love seeing our patches everywhere. There's something so cool about being with a bunch of women just doing our thing.

The primary reason that most women join a single-sex group is for the social connection and the unique dynamics that occur when men are absent. I witness many knowing glances and quite a few high-fives as I watch a gathering cheer for each other as they tackle a new challenge or hang by a campfire, sharing stories of learning to ride and the mistakes made while improving their skills. Many women describe a feeling of intimidation around men, a subtle pressure to keep up or not embarrass themselves that fades when the men disappear. By venturing off with other women, female riders often build the confidence they need to return to mixed-gender groups, bringing that feeling of support with them.

Women may also mention the downside to some groups: drama. For these riders, finding the right group of women to share their adventures with is as important as being with other females. Too much drama and not enough riding, and they were off in search of different crowds or to start their own networks with more laid-back attitudes and "let's keep the focus on fun" rules for behavior. Many women I've met belong to more than one group, some single-sex and others mixed, thus satisfying a variety of desires for connection and community.

My first experience riding with any type of group was through three mountain passes with a break for lunch in the middle. I'd only dated my now-husband for just a few weeks when he invited me to join him and three of his friends; I'd be on the back of his bike as pillion. The group had ridden together numerous times and quickly fell into a rhythm that they all understood: how to communicate, when to pass, who led, and who rode sweep. They all knew the restaurant where we'd be meeting for lunch should someone need to stop before then and catch up later. They were efficient, had similar styles, and felt very comfortable with one

Part of the draw of joining a group is the social aspect.

We started the group only a year ago, and this was our first major event: camping and riding together. It was absolutely incredible to see this many women, all on bikes, lined up and ready to ride. Following them as sweep, I felt a rush of pride in all of us as I watched them motoring down the road in unison. It was a sense of sisterhood, of community, of solidarity. I can't really put it into words.

another. I learned several things about groups on that ride, with probably the most important lesson being to never leave my cell phone on the table when going to the restroom. The pictures they took in my absence, while definitely not up to the standards of obscene, certainly met the criteria for ridiculous. It took another ride with a different group of people to realize what else I had learned that day: that I like going fast and I really dislike being dependent on others when their style of riding is radically different from mine.

We participated in another organized ride a few weeks later, and it was then that I came to understand the differences in dynamics between groups. A work friend of my husband invited us to join her riding cohorts for a day trip to a nearby national park. We met everyone at a ferry terminal, and, after introductions, we rode across Puget Sound together. The bikes quickly got into formation, two-by-two in slightly staggered rows, and rumbled off onto the local roads at speeds barely reaching the posted limit. The other motorcycles were primarily cruisers, with much smaller fuel tanks than ours, necessitating a gas stop within what seemed to me a very short

Look for a group of women who share your riding style and interests.

Motorcycling friends become like family, and all members are welcome!

distance. Several riders took a smoke break while we were stopped, and after ten or fifteen minutes, we were once again on the road. Next up was a lunch stop at a popular Mexican restaurant, which with at least twenty riders to order, eat, and pay, was a lengthy meal. The conversations were engaging, the people were very welcoming, and everyone had interesting stories to tell.

A lot of laughs later, with stomachs full and tanks topped off, we headed up the twisty mountain road to our destination. The group stayed together for the entire fifteen miles, in formation, until we reached the top and parked. After I got off the bike and removed my helmet, I sidled up to my husband and whispered in his ear, "These are great people to chat with and get to know, but don't ever make me ride that slowly again." He nodded in full agreement. Citing obligations back at home early in the evening, we bade farewell at the turnoff for the return ferry while the group headed off to yet another gas station. We then picked up the pace and had a lively ride back home.

Women create a sisterhood: mentoring, respecting different levels of ability, being more accepting and less judgmental. There's a lot of sharing of tips and safety advice and a lot of high-fives and laughter.

When I used to arrive at coed events, especially on my sport bike, the men would gape at me as if I were an oddity. It's really nice to ride with women who just see me as normal.

At the same time I was discovering that I wasn't a group ride rider, I learned that I am a group joiner. As a member of the Iron Butt Association, I love riding to meet friends all over the country, hanging out with them for a short lunch, an overnight tire-kicking session, or a long weekend gathering with a lot of tall tales, laughter, and more than a few beers. When I was invited to a weekend campout with a women's riding group, I had a wonderful time pitching my tent near others I barely knew, riding to a local drive-in movie theater together a few blocks away to sit on the grass and catch a film while reminiscing about my childhood spent at such places, and sharing a bottle of wine later at the campsite. These are people I want to get to know better: bright, interesting, and fun women who are dedicated to riding. I liked the absence of men and the different energy with which we surrounded ourselves. I just don't want to ride in formation with them. Luckily, I have that choice because I can meet them at our destination and still be part of the group.

Over the years, I have come to realize that not all groups are created equal, and what works well for one person may not hold the slightest attraction to another. I'm glad I have had the opportunity to discover my preferences for myself, not based on how my husband or my friends choose to ride. I realized early on that I do not like being confined to the timelines of others, that I am uncomfortable riding with large numbers of other bikes, and that I like the flexibility of making last-minute deviations to plans. What I also learned is that I am not an isolationist: I come alive with others, and I love sharing adventures and a good story with a group of fellow motorcyclists.

Women riders form strong bonds and friendships.

Group events offer many opportunities for participation as either a rider or an organizer.

The critical element is for each person to have the freedom to discover how, or even if, being part of a group is right for her. Many riders who prefer heading out on the road alone still enjoy sharing time and swapping tips and tidbits with others who understand their passion. Having a motorcycling community, whether in person or online, can provide valuable support when questions arise or bikes break down. I'm amazed at the willingness of strangers to jump in and offer mechanical expertise, bike towing, meals for hungry riders, and even a bed for the night, all because we share a love of riding. Meeting these strangers who quickly become friends is, for almost all the people with whom I speak about riding, one of the best parts of motorcycling. For most, getting involved, giving back, and mentoring new riders brings far greater personal satisfaction than the time and effort it takes.

What works best for you? Are you a joiner who relishes connections with others? If you are inclined to be in community with fellow riders, how often

Contrary to popular opinion, I found that when I rode with groups of men, they always wanted to spend time talking about their bikes. With the women I've met, it's "Let's go! Let's get out and ride!"

I saw a huge group ride past while I was stopped by the side of the road. It was a total testosterone-fest: going way over the speed limit, popping wheelies, and showing off. It freaked me out! No way did I ever want to ride with a group of guys like that. I like riding a sport bike, but with women it's just different: more about the ride than the machismo.

do you want to get together, with how many people, and for what purpose? Is a face-to-face meeting important, or is an online chat sufficient? Is your primary interest to socialize, to pound out the miles, or a combination of both? Are you an organizer, or would you rather simply show up and follow someone else's lead? Are you more of a loner who wants a place to get information but, otherwise, is happy doing her own thing? Or perhaps, like me, you prefer riding with one or two friends, or even alone, but join groups for social events and competitions.

Ask Your Dealer

Ask your dealer if they host or know of activities for riders, especially in the dreary winter months when most riders opt to park their bikes, thus giving you an opportunity to meet others who share a common interest.

Groups exist to meet a wide variety of interests, and when a new need emerges, it seems as if a group always pops up to satisfy that need. Ranging from local to regional to worldwide, the variety of riding communities can be staggering. Some people gather weekly for breakfast and stories but ride very few actual miles together. Others barely know each other in their street clothes, stopping only long enough to decide who is leading and who is riding sweep before taking off for a challenging ride through the countryside and waving good-bye as they turn toward home at the end of the day. Meet-up groups may have as few as twenty or more than a thousand members who post rides, host barbecues, and hold annual campouts, diversifying their activities to meet the needs of their particular population. Same-sex groups, singles groups, couples-only groups, groups for enthusiasts of particular brands of motorcycle, sport riders, adventure riders, long-distance riders—there's something for anyone looking to connect.

I know women who have checked out a variety of riding groups, both female-only and mixed-gender, and have not found the perfect fit for whatever reason. As such, they have opted to create their own circles to better meet their needs. Most started in a similar fashion: wanting someone with whom to share their interests, gathering a few like-minded souls, and recruiting friends. One woman

All Kinds of Groups

National and international organizations come in all shapes, sizes, sexual orientations, and faiths and often have local chapters and regional events to bring riders together. Many groups combine riding with service, supporting either a specific charity or outreach in general. Here's just a sampling of some of the many groups out there:

Christian Motorcyclists Association: **www.cmausa.org**

Desmo Owners Club (Ducati): **www.ducatiusa.com**

Dykes on Bikes Women's Motorcycle Contingent: **www.dykesonbikes.org**

Harley Owners Group (HOG): **_www.hog.com_**

International Fellowship of Motorcycling Rotarians: **www.ifmr.org**

Jewish Motorcyclists Alliance: **www.jewishmotorcyclistsalliance.org**

Leather and Lace: **www.leatherandlacemc.com**

Motor Maids: **www.motormaids.org**

Women's International Motorcycling Association: **www.wimaworld.com**

Women in the Wind: **www.womeninthewind.org**

Women on Wheels: **www.womenonwheels.org**

described her inability to find other females whose passion was adventure riding, so she started her own network, The Dirty Girls. Groups with names like Desert Dames, Headlights, and Dangerous Curves have proliferated in local riding areas. Many groups join with other groups for camp-ins or ride-ins, providing the opportunity to meet a larger network of women riders from all over the country. Some groups are Facebook-based, some are open to anyone, and still others are by invitation only.

As with so many aspects of motorcycling, the Internet is your friend: a good search engine is the place to start your research. You can find websites that connect you with groups in your area; from there, you can explore which ones might be worth checking out. I've found sites that simply post listings of all the gatherings in an area, while others categorize groups by highly detailed criteria, such as model of bike or style of riding. Contact group leaders with any questions you might have, give a few of their events a try, and see if their group is the right place for you.

Bikers arrive for a July 4 ride to support several military charities.

Charity Rides

Charity rides bring together groups of motorcyclists who share a desire to support a common cause by heading out on the road together. Some require participants to donate or raise money, while others welcome riders to join in for the sense of community and camaraderie. Some are scavenger hunt-style events, some are large group rides, and still others are conducted as poker runs.

Some fundraising rides are targeted specifically to women, both as riders and as beneficiaries. For example, the Sweeties on Wheelies group benefits the Women's Resource Center of Wyoming, and the Soroptimist International Club of Trenton, Michigan, sponsors a "Save the Girls" group ride. The Diva Angels, a nationwide group, have an annual event that supports several organizations, including Special Olympics and the Susan G. Komen Foundation. The Sturgis Buffalo Chip's Biker Belles, a Harley Davidson-focused group, started with two goals in mind: to raise awareness of and support for women who ride and to raise money for charities of particular interest to women. Every year, during the Sturgis rally, the Belles gather to share stories, listen to inspiring speakers, and donate to a cause. While technically not a ride, the gathering brings together women united in their passion for motorcycling to benefit common causes. More information about events of particular interest to women can be found through websites such as Women Riders Now (www.womenridersnow.com).

The majority of charity rides are open to both sexes. The Tour of Honor Ride, for example, takes place over an entire riding season. Motorcyclists ride to memorials and monuments that honor veterans throughout the entire fifty states, documenting their visits by taking photographs of the monuments with a rally flag and, if possible, their bikes. The Ride to the Wall, or Rolling Thunder Ride for Freedom, aims to raise awareness about prisoners of war and service members still missing in action from any and all American military conflicts. This memorial ride, which includes more than 400,000 participants, starts at the Pentagon and finishes at the Vietnam Veterans Memorial.

For those attending the Sturgis Motorcycle Rally, there are two charity rides during the annual gathering. The Mayor's Ride benefits both the Sturgis Volunteer Fire Department and Sturgis Police Reserve, while the Legends Ride splits its donations between the Black Hills Special Olympics and the Sturgis Motorcycle Museum and Hall of Fame.

The Kyle Petty Charity Ride Across America raises money for Victory Junction and other children's charities. This cross-country ride combines sponsors, motorcycle enthusiasts, fans, and celebrities to bring awareness to the needs of children both nationally and within their local communities.

America's 9/11 Ride follows roads from Shanksville, Pennsylvania, to the Pentagon and finishes at the site of the World Trade Center. Motorcyclists can join along the route or complete the entire journey. The ride serves as a remembrance

Motorcyclists turned out in large numbers for the 9/11 memorial Iron and Steel run from New York City to Arlington, Virginia.

for those who lost their lives in the attacks of September 11, 2001, while also honoring and celebrating first responders currently active across the United States. Riders can choose to contribute to America's 9/11 Foundation in lieu of entry fees.

There are many smaller events benefitting local charities around the country. Ride for Kids is a series of rides throughout the country benefiting the Pediatric Brain Tumor Foundation. The MS5000 was started to raise awareness and funds for the Multiple Sclerosis Society. Eddie's Road, named after Eddie James, funds local projects around the country that help abused youth successfully bridge the gap between foster care and adulthood. The Chick Run Association of Grand Rapids, Michigan, holds an annual ride to benefit local women's charities in addition to supporting women-owned businesses along the route. The Lady Riders of Western Washington put together a calendar to raise money for the Crisis Clinic. As you can imagine, the list goes on, and more events continue to pop up.

Riding in formation during a poker run in Memphis, Tennessee.

Poker runs are an increasingly popular way to bring together motorcyclists and charities, with entry fees donated to the charity that the sponsoring group has chosen to support. Starting at a common location, riders are given a score sheet and specific directions to five to seven checkpoints. Riders receive a playing card at each stop, which is noted on their score sheets. At the final stop, just as in poker, the player with the best hand wins.

Many group rides are not fundraisers but are held to remember or celebrate significant events in our history. These commemorative rides either visit sites en masse or invite riders to plan routes on their own. One such ride, the Trail of Tears Remembrance Ride, is a four-day event through eight states commemorating the forced relocation of Native Americans from the eastern United States to reservations west of the Mississippi. These migrations of the Cherokee, Seminole, Chickasaw, Choctaw, and Creek nations, among others, occurred between the 1820s and 1840s. This ride is one of the largest in North America.

Attending events as a member of the Iron Butt Association, I've met several individual riders with remarkable personal stories. Paul was a dedicated competitive long-distance motorcyclist when he began experiencing fatigue and muscle weakness. A diagnosis of multiple sclerosis soon followed, which, for many, might signal an end to riding. In Paul's case, however, it gave birth to a personal quest to raise awareness and money for the MS Society in an effort to help find a cure for all who are faced with the devastating disease. Combining his passion for riding with an even greater passion for his mission, he created his Endless Road Tour: he has challenged himself to ride one million miles, giving speeches to any group willing to hear his story. Spreading awareness further, he has initiated several online-supported rallies, including the MS5000, where riders around the world can participate, riding in their own areas and raising funds for the MS Society.

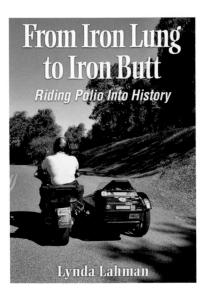

After writing my first book, *Two-Up: Navigating a Relationship 1,000 Miles at a Time*, I was approached by a friend to write his story of growing up with the effects of polio and the worldwide efforts to eradicate the disease. What made his tale unique was his dedication to spreading the word of the work of The Rotary Foundation's Polio Plus project. Bob, who has only ever walked with leg braces and crutches, was able to start motorcycling at thirteen when his father attached a sidecar to a Honda 50. He started the No Polio Rally, an eight- to twelve-hour fun rally, in his hometown of Folsom, California, to bring awareness to other riders and raise money for Rotary. He has ridden across the United States, Canada, and Australia, giving talks to Rotary groups and the media along the way. All of the proceeds from the book *From Iron Lung to Iron Butt: Riding Polio into History* go directly to the Polio Plus fund, matched two-to-one by the Bill and Melinda Gates Foundation.

Prior to meeting Paul and Bob, it hadn't occurred to me that a person could combine motorcycle riding and charity on an individual level, let alone create rallies and events to bring others into the fold. I'd heard of solo runners or bicyclists who had traversed the country for some cause. Despite being a runner, I never really thought about doing something like that myself—I was the one doing the donating, not the one going all out. I have no idea why I was so shortsighted, but once I was exposed to the concept, it made complete sense:

> *"I was once told a cure for MS was a million miles away, so I figured I would just go and get it and bring it back."*
> —Longhaulpaul 2012

take your passion—in this case, riding—and find a way to use it to help a cause about which you care deeply. I have since learned there are countless others using their passion for motorcycling as fundraisers for organizations and individuals in need.

If you are interested in starting a charity ride, whether to complete individually or organize as a group effort, there are websites offering information that will help you learn how to get something going. "Guerrilla Fundraising: How to Ride for a Cause, Fundraising beyond the Poker Run" on the website Women Riders Now (www.womenridersnow. com) is one such article with valuable tips and suggestions.

I have found the motorcycling community to be generous with time and knowledge. If you are willing to ask, there is probably someone willing to step up and point you in the right direction. Putting together your own ride requires tremendous energy and dedication, but raising money, arranging speaking engagements, coordinating places to stay, setting up funding pages, and establishing a social media presence naturally brings you in touch with others. Even if you ride solo, you will be creating a community that connects you with others who share or support your passion. My friendships with Paul and Bob have proved to me that the effort is worth it.

International Female Ride Day

Started in 2007 by Vicki Gray to highlight the number of women who ride, International Female Ride Day (IFRD) has grown exponentially in the ensuing years thanks to social media and support from women around the world. Vicki, a riding instructor, former Supersport racer, and now vintage bike racer, founded Race Girl Motorsports to support women and riding. She is now the voice behind Motoress.com, a website devoted to all aspects of women's motorcycling. IFRD's mission is to increase public awareness of women who ride and to encourage those females who have yet to take up the sport.

I first learned about IFRD when I happened to stop at a BMW dealer for a minor repair and was invited to attend their event on the first Saturday of May, which happened to be the next weekend. The dealership hosted demonstration rides of the Zero, a new electric motorcycle; provided delicious food; and invited various women's groups to set up booths to share their information with the crowds who stopped by. Conversations were lively as the more experienced riders shared their stories about why they rode, their preferred motorcycles, and some of their thrills and spills with the newcomers, encouraging those who were thinking about getting started. The sense of community was strong, and the experienced women riders' willingness to help beginners get into the sport was exciting to witness. Women learned about groups to join, classes to take, and where to purchase riding gear made for them. Many participants exchanged phone numbers and e-mail addresses and even found new friends with whom to ride. The success of Vicki's vision was very apparent everywhere I looked that day.

Motorcycle Rallies

"Been to Sturgis?" I, along with almost anyone who rides any model or brand of bike anywhere, have been asked that question by virtually everyone, including strangers at gas stations and fast-food restaurants. My answer is no, that although the Sturgis Motorcycle Rally is not my cup of tea, it is the premier happening for many of my friends and obviously for many thousands of other riders throughout the world. It is a Harley-Davidson event, and it is probably one of the best-known rallies anywhere. Early each August, bikes converge on Sturgis, Wyoming, for a bit of riding and a lot of ogling of full-dress and chopped Harleys in addition to scantily clad bodies, blocks upon blocks of vendors offering everything from custom tattoos to custom parts, world-class concerts, and general merrymaking at all hours of the day and night. Bikers start arriving at the normally quiet town weeks ahead of the action, looking for places to camp or rooms to rent, doing whatever they can to find a space to sleep, hang out, and share good times with fellow enthusiasts. For many Harley riders, it is akin to a rite of passage that one must experience at least once during their lifetime; for others, it becomes an annual pilgrimage for rekindling old friendships and creating new ones.

Whether for a once-in-a-lifetime visit or as part of an annual tradition, Harley riders fill the town of Sturgis each August.

Most motorcycle brands have owners' organizations that support and encourage connections within their communities. For example, Harley-Davidson has the Harley Owners Group (HOG); BMW has the BMW Motorcycle Owners of America (BMW-MOA); and Honda has the Gold Wing Road Riders Association and the CB1000R Owners Club, to name only a few. Many of these organizations sponsor annual rallies where riders, vendors, manufacturers, and a multitude of others gather to swap stories, listen to great speakers, and generally have a lively time meeting riders old and new who share their passion. Shopping stalls abound with clothing and gear, training sessions take place in large parking lots, seminars bring the latest information on equipment and safety, adventurers share stories of their travels, bands play into the night, and riders head off in all directions during the day to explore the roads in a new playground. These are social events, not competitive rallies. They're rich resources about your particular make of bike, one-stop shopping venues for parts and accessories, opportunities to sit on and demo new models, and opportunities to introduce yourself to a wide variety of motorcyclists, all in one place.

BMW-MOA hosts an annual rally in rotating locations around North America, as does the Gold Wing Road Riders Association. In addition, BMW, Honda, Ducati, and numerous other motorcycle brands host regional rallies with the intention of bringing together riders, both individuals and clubs, to get to know

A look at Sturgis's main street during the annual rally.

each other in an informal setting. Many of these smaller rallies also offer seminars and riding courses as well as local maps to inspire those unfamiliar with the area to get out on their bikes and explore great roads.

Adventure enthusiasts can meet up with other like-minded riders at rallies such as the KTM Adventure Rider Rally or the GS Giants' Stampede. These gatherings, like others, combine seminars, clinics, food, and fun, bringing people together to learn, ride, and share their passion for off-road riding. The focus of these rallies is to get riders on their bikes and out into adventures. Riders primarily interested in sport touring can seek out events such as the Motorcycle Sport Touring Associations' Rendezvous (STAR), where the focus is on those who want to meet up with others to ride rather than shop or take seminars.

Whether on your own, with a partner, or with a group, touring on a motorcycle lets you fully experience the sights around you.

Motorcycle Tours

You can find motorcycle touring companies all over the world, and they are ready to supply you with a bike, a guide, a great itinerary, and all of your hotel and meal reservations. All you have to do is show up, gear up, grab your keys, and follow your leader. The tour operators provide supply vans to carry your luggage, allowing you to carry street clothes for evenings out on the town, and they will also transport you to dinner if you prefer to drink a glass of wine and not drive. Tours can be on- or off-road and range from weekends to several weeks in duration. Some cater exclusively to riders of a certain make of motorcycle, others to adventure riders, and still others to those interested in long-distance journeys. Many of the same companies offer self-guided tours, where the route and hotel stays are coordinated for you, and you head out on your own to ride at your own pace and without a group of other motorcyclists as companions. Whether on your own or with a group, you get the fun of riding without the hassle of logistics and without having to ship your bike to far corners of the globe. However, if you prefer your own bike to a rental, the tour company can often help arrange the shipping.

Online Forums

As with almost any interest you might pursue in today's connected world, there is an entire motorcycling community online in the form of virtual clubs and forums. If you can't find the niche you want, you can always start your own group!

Some forums are open to anyone interested in joining, while others are invitation-only. Groups might be limited to a single subject or may have a wide variety of subtopics. Many, such as the FJR forum (www.fjrforum.com), appeal to a single style of motorcycle but are open to any rider; owning the bike isn't a requirement. During the Iron Butt Rally, for example, the FJR forum is one of the most popular sites for following and commenting on the rally, and long-distance enthusiasts of all stripes and bikes eagerly check updates during the eleven-day event. Such online groups permit those who weren't selected for entry into the rally, or who opt to watch from the comfort of home, to feel part of the excitement, which is what some of the best forums can do: bring you along as part of the group.

Whether curious about adventure riding or passionate about the track, you can find a forum to learn more or share your knowledge with others who are starting out. The Motorcycle Tourer's Forum (www.mctourer.com) is tailored to those interested in, as the name implies, motorcycle touring. Sport tourers may find camaraderie with fellow enthusiasts on the Sport Touring Association's site (www.sport-touring.net). Harley fans can check out sites such as HD Forums (www.hdforums.com), Harley-Davidson Forums (www.harley-davidsonforums.com), or the V-Twin Forum (www.v-twinforum.com) to name just a few of the dozens to choose from.

Forums, for the most part, are simply places to discuss ideas and chat with others, but, on occasion, one or two extremely opinionated members can hijack a conversation and turn a benign discussion into something quite heated. I tend to shy away from fueling the flames when I see a discussion going downhill, and I quietly step aside if things start getting nasty. Most forums are owned and overseen by a moderator who

Consider the Source

Although online forums are a great resource, remember that the Internet does not provide all of the answers, all of the time. Just because someone has 50,000 posts does not mean that the person knows what he or she is talking about.

Websites and Magazines

In addition to general-interest motorcycling websites, there are sites specifically dedicated to women's riding. Offering tips, news, event listings, and advertisements geared toward female motorcyclists, these sites can be valuable resources for riders both new and experienced. Most have blogs and forums where you can ask questions, get advice, and connect with others. Motoress (www.motoress.com) and Women Riders Now (www.womenridersnow.com) have extensive menus ranging from shopping to safety, as does the Women Motorcyclist (www.womenmotorcyclist.com) site. Gear Chic (www.gearchic.com) primarily focuses on women's riding gear while addressing other questions and issues that women face in the world of motorcycling. Her Motorcycle (www.her-motorcycle.com) and Harley-Davidson Women Riders (click on "Women" under the "Community" tab at www.harley-davidson.com) are just a few of many others devoted to women and motorcycling.

Motorcycling magazines often have print and digital components for today's readers. *Cycle World*, *American Motorcyclist*, *Rider*, and *Motorcyclist* are examples of general motorcycling magazines. *Motorcycle Consumer News* offers reviews of new bike models as well as articles focused on safe riding. The *Iron Butt Magazine* targets the long-distance motorcycling community, while *Dirt Rider* and *Sport Rider* are geared toward their specific interest groups. There are a plethora of brand-focused magazines, such as *HOG Tales*, *American Iron*, and *American Rider*, which cater to Harley-Davidson enthusiasts. Dealers often have copies of a variety of these publications, allowing you to browse before you subscribe.

For those interested in finding great roads to ride, *RoadRUNNER* and *Backroads* magazines offer ride reports accompanied by stunning photographs and maps with highlighted routes to try. Organizations such as the BMW Motorcycle Owners Association publish magazines that feature stories about their brands, often including articles about beautiful roads and the adventures of riders who have explored them. BMW in particular includes both on- and off-road stories because their bikes target both audiences.

makes valiant attempts to enforce a modicum of decency and will often ban someone who continually starts arguments. Women-only forums may make you feel more comfortable about sharing without fearing judgments from others.

Even if you aren't a joiner and don't see yourself becoming part of a riding group, these forums provide valuable resources as well a wealth of opinions that may be incredibly informative or, occasionally, less than helpful. I've noticed over the years that the online activity tends to quiet down in the summer months, when everyone's out on the road, and pick up in the winter months, when everyone's starting to go stir crazy while waiting for riding season to resume.

Mentoring New Riders

Once you progress from a novice rider to an experienced motorcyclist, you may want to explore the idea of giving back to the motorcycling community and bringing other women into the fold. I often reflect on the women who supported and encouraged me when I first got on the bike as pillion and then transitioned to solo rider. While my husband was an incredible teacher and mentor,

Whether teaching a course or mentoring another rider, there many ways to pay it forward to new female riders.

these female riders understood some of the pressures I felt internally and the expectations I put on myself as well as some of my fears and insecurities that he couldn't relate to. Through sharing stories, laughter, and camaraderie, I felt part of a larger sisterhood that helped me gain confidence even when I had my doubts. I am a firm believer in paying it forward, and mentoring others is a large part of the positive obligation I feel I owe those who came before me.

I enjoy attending a number of motorcycling activities and often meet up with friends when I do. In fact, reconnecting with others from around the country and even around the world is one of my main reasons for going to many events. It's easy when I arrive to find my "group" and hang out. There's a lot to catch up on, adventures and photos to share, and a comfort in relaxing with people I already know. Despite being outgoing, I am also a bit shy, and meeting strangers can sometimes feel awkward and exhausting.

But then I think about the times I've been the newcomer, the one standing hesitantly at the side of the room, not knowing where to sit or looking for another person standing alone who might be open to conversation. That feeling of isolation is far worse than any discomfort I might have about introducing myself to someone I don't know in a place where I am already familiar. I don't want anyone to perceive the sport I love, or me, as cliquey. Besides, everyone has a story to tell, and the new faces in the room are the friends I have yet to meet. Expanding the tent, growing the family, and bringing along the newcomers is part of my mantra.

I seek out newcomers, especially women, at all of the events I attend. I don't care whether they are pillions or riders. In long-distance circles, the female presence is still small enough that it's always nice to meet more women. In situations where I am the new face, I take a deep breath, walk up to strangers, and introduce myself. We all have motorcycling in common; therefore, we have a built-in conversation starter. I've sought out activities that might be appealing to newer riders even though I may be far more experienced, and I've participated just to lend a hand. My role isn't to be the expert but to be the friend, the one who invites the person on the fringes to come into the circle. I am amazed at how many friendships have developed from such a simple beginning step. I am also pleased to see so many other women doing the same, welcoming new female riders with open arms, high fives, and cheers.

Many beginning motorcyclists are seeking other women to ride with but often don't know how or where to find them. Participating in group rides, stopping by dealerships and talking with salespeople, and staying connected through online forums are some of the ways you can keep a pulse on who is just getting started and might want a riding buddy. Offering to go out for a few hours with someone who wants to build her skills can boost the confidence of a novice immensely. Leading

You can find all kinds of friends in motorcycling circles.

There's nothing like the feeling of adventure and accomplishment after a successful ride.

small group outings and coordinating them to meet the needs of those still learning can teach valuable lessons regarding safety when riding with others.

I remember my time in parking lots and on quiet back roads and greatly appreciated those who were willing to hang out with me when I simply needed a friendly face and supportive company. I wasn't yet ready to go out alone, and having a friend go with me meant the difference between thinking about riding and actually riding. Even today, when I have a new bike to ride or a new road to test out, it's nice to have a girlfriend go with me for moral support and usually a stop for coffee or lunch, making it a social experience. That support feels so welcoming to a new rider.

Contributing a woman's voice to online forums adds an important perspective to what is often a male-dominated conversation. Many of the women I know are as opinionated as their male counterparts, and having them show up online reminds other female riders that we are out there in growing numbers. If you are confident regarding mechanics or GPS use, or you have strong views about the best oil or which tire you prefer, displaying that knowledge publicly invites women to become more involved in the care and maintenance of their own bikes. Whether on a forum devoted to a female audience or a more general forum, taking the time to read and comment may encourage others to jump in as well.

Not all women like shopping; I'm not a fan myself, but I do enjoy sharing the experience with a girlfriend. It's nice to get another rider's opinion about gear, fit, and quality. My riding group and I occasionally borrow each other's jackets or pants to see how they feel on a long ride before plunking down a small fortune for something we need. We compare stories of leaking seams and walking distances in motorcycling boots, and we share tips for keeping cool in the summer and warm when it's cold. When I was a novice, I had no idea what questions to ask, let alone where to shop and what was considered a decent fit. My husband, while extremely encouraging about my need for gear, wasn't a helpful shopping companion other than having strong opinions about what he deemed safe. Style wasn't an issue for him, but it was one of the more important considerations for me. Offering to go shopping with a newcomer to the sport is a great way to show support and to make it a fun part of riding while ensuring that she learns what to look for in protective gear. Even online research can be overwhelming, so simply sitting with a new rider and sorting out all the information that's out there can be immeasurably helpful for her.

Shopping for gear can be more fun with a friend.

Some women may be intimidated about taking a new-rider course or going back to take an intermediate course. Or perhaps someone wants to venture off-road or give the track a try, but she feels a bit uneasy and is not quite sure if she is ready. Offering to take a class with a friend may help her overcome her hesitation; in the process, you will most likely learn something new, too. For me, seeing things through a new lens almost always opens my eyes to a new perspective, and listening to an instructor teaching something with which I am already familiar usually reminds me of details I've forgotten. In addition, if I take a class with a friend, she and I now have a common language when we go out riding together, having heard the same things at the same time. We can practice the exercises we did in the class, and I am no longer the "expert" but just another student working on my own techniques. Just as I have pointers to share with her, she now has insights to offer to me as well, and that can certainly help boost her confidence.

Track days provide opportunities to invite a street-riding friend to join you, whether she feels ready to go out on the tarmac yet or not. The thought of getting on the oval and accelerating around the turns may be terrifying to someone who has yet to set foot on a track, but with encouragement and some good instruction, she may find her inner speed demon. Even if she realizes that it's not for her, what she learns will help her when she gets back on the street. Do you know women who would benefit from a personal request to accompany you and perhaps even take a spin? If so, take the time to extend the invitation. It's all about inclusion and bringing new riders into the sport.

Not everything to do with motorcycling involves getting on the bike and riding. During the winter months, some dealerships offer seminars and guest speakers. Often, these presentations include personal stories of adventure, accompanied by beautiful photographs and amusing anecdotes. While your friend may still decide riding isn't for her, she may come to better understand and support your passion.

Many Harley-Davidson showrooms have women's "Garage Parties," where new and potential riders can ask questions, learn some basics, and meet others in a female-only environment. These are popular events and opportunities to invite friends who may be considering riding—particularly Harleys—to join you and introduce them to others who could become part of their riding family in the future.

The entry-level ride for those interested in joining the Iron Butt Association is typically a SaddleSore, or 1,000 miles in twenty-four hours. Many of those who desire their certificate and membership number will attempt this ride on their own, but an equal number will ride their first one with a friend or mentor. A crucial consideration when deciding on going with someone else is determining who and what sets the pace for the ride. It's not about speed: you need to average less than 45 miles per hour to finish, which is an easy pace on most interstates

Some accessories are just for fun.

if you are efficient with your food and gas breaks. During most of my long rides, I've had plenty of time to stop and sleep for several hours and still finish with time to spare. Some groups, like the Motorcycle Tourer's Forum, sponsor SaddleSore rides in various parts of the country, providing preplanned routes and witnesses to sign your starting and finishing forms. Volunteering to be a witness, or even to ride with someone, can be a lot of fun and a great way to encourage someone to give it a try. If choosing to accompany someone on the ride, be sure to go at the pace of the slowest rider and have an exit plan if, for any reason, one of you needs to stop. If you are mentoring a rider who is new to long-distance rides, your job is to support her ride; if you are attempting your own SaddleSore, it's best to go solo rather than bring along a newbie.

Like any new endeavor, many novices start out with enthusiasm, but some may soon feel isolated and discouraged if unable to find others with whom to share their interest, leading them to eventually abandon the sport. Including newer riders on poker runs, rides to eat, rallies, and other social gatherings, and introducing them to others at these get-togethers, will help connect them to the riding community. Building friendships with women motorcyclists is an important part of making positive connections, and bringing them into the sisterhood offers tremendous satisfaction as you help support women being safe, competent, and confident on the road.

Growing the Sport

I work with athletes, helping them learn the mental skills necessary for being successful in their endeavors. When I first start out with new clients, I ask them why they are doing their particular sport, what they love about it, and what they would miss the most if they were forced to quit. I want to understand the source of their passion—what excites them and motivates them to keep practicing. What does this have to do with motorcycling?

If we want any sport to continue to attract participants, we need to keep bringing new people into the fold, inviting them to give it a try, and supporting them as they take their first steps. If we want manufacturers to give more consideration to the challenges that women riders face, we need to keep growing our presence as consumers. Clothing makers will offer more choices when they have more buyers for their wares. Motorcycle magazines will feature an increasing number of articles appealing to both sexes and more photographs of competent, athletic female riders and fewer centerfold wannabes. More women riding equates to a greater female voice in all aspects of the sport.

What brought you into motorcycling? Was it something you saw or read? Was it a person who invited you for a ride? Is there something that inspired you and encouraged you to hop on a bike? How can you pay it forward, bringing someone new into the community of women riders? Can you talk about your passion with those who will listen or post photographs of some of your most amazing rides on social media? In conversations with friends and strangers who so freely share their fears about the dangers of riding, can you listen respectfully and then offer your perspective without becoming defensive or dismissive, instead explaining what you do to stay safe so they might reconsider their position?

I am still surprised by the number of people who approach me and are startled to see me on my own motorcycle. When I tell them that I compete in long-distance

events and describe the number of miles I put on my bike in a day, a week, or a year, their jaws often drop. "Oh, I could never do that!" is a common response. "I'm too old, too short, too whatever." When I tell them my age, they are even more astonished, as if I am doing something remarkable. "I always thought it'd be fun to ride a motorcycle, but (fill in the excuse). It's so courageous of you that you're doing it." Nonriders need to become aware that women are out on the roads in significant numbers, on all manner of bikes, at all ages, and having a blast. I'm not doing anything out of the ordinary; I'm not unique or particularly daring—I'm merely a competent woman pursuing something I love. I am constantly reminding women that if motorcycling has ever been a dream of theirs, then what are they waiting for?

Invite and encourage those who have always dreamed of riding to take a class and see for themselves if it's right for them rather than just continue to praise those they deem brave enough to go for it. Talk to those who think that motorcycling is the latest fad for women and encourage them to think a bit further about what goes into being a good rider. Share why it's worth it to learn correctly, find others who ride, and join the community of women on the road. Challenge them to dig deep and experience what riding has to offer. In all situations, support their journey, and perhaps a few new riders will emerge from your efforts.

Posting on social media about great rides, club events, and your riding community may elicit curiosity from peers who aren't familiar with the

Women riders are a significant presence at the Indianapolis Pride Parade.

Be Cool

I've heard female riders describe other women who've voiced their admiration: "Your leathers are so cool, and your bike is awesome. I should get one!" While we want to encourage new enthusiasts, it's also important to separate those who see motorcycling as the latest fashion statement from those who are serious about learning to ride safely and competently. Riding is cool, but it also takes work, dedication, and attention.

motorcycling aspect of your life. Coworkers may see your gear in a pile in a corner of your cubicle when they stop by for a chat, but do they know that you fly around the track in your free time or that you rode a thousand miles over the weekend to meet a few friends for lunch?

What keeps you riding? For many, the friendships formed are almost as important as the riding itself. Do you have friends you'd love to see at some of your group campouts and poker runs? Would you be willing to take a class with one of your girlfriends or have her ride pillion to an event with you to see what it's like? Or even invite her to come to an event in a car so that she can get a feel for the fun and camaraderie you experience; perhaps she will be able to picture herself on a bike next time. Bring a friend to a track day and let her witness the thrill of speed and the sights and sounds of other women racing around the turns. She may come in contact with her inner racer and want to learn to ride herself.

Rallies are a great way to share your passion with friends. Camping, concerts, and food vendors, not to mention shopping and beer gardens, highlight the social aspects of motorcycling. Listening to speakers describing incredible roads, breathtaking scenery, and the remote towns and villages they've visited may capture the imagination of someone who has always dreamed of travel. Realizing the intimacy of exploring all the corners of the world on two wheels may fuel her desire to get out there herself.

Writing articles and blogs about your adventures can inspire others to step outside their comfort zones, perhaps encouraging a street rider to attempt dirt or a Sunday-only group member to venture out for a track day. I started writing for *Iron Butt Magazine* after I noticed in their premier issue that there were no articles about pillions. For the first few years, my column was called Pillion's Perspective, and when I switched to riding my own bike, we simply changed the title to Perspectives. I have the freedom to write about anything that interests me, and my hope is to inspire women, in particular, to get on the bike if they aren't already. It matters little whether they are on the back or front seat.

Magazines welcome contributions from female readers. Most don't pay, but you are spreading the word and offering a woman's perspective in what is a milieu often dominated by men. We may ride as far, as fast, and as hard as our male counterparts, but our stories are unique and deserve a voice. Women reading the words of other women feel more included and more inclined to see themselves in the motorcycling world. By being able to picture herself on the bike, taking off, and creating her own adventures, you may just entice one more woman to ride.

While you are out there looking for ways to grow our sport, it's also imperative to combat misinformation and misperceptions. For example, in the long-distance community, a very common mistake made by many journalists is to call a long-distance rally a race when it definitely is not. Why does it matter? Because it may discourage some riders from giving long-distance riding even a cursory glance. The same with sport riders: only a very tiny percentage of riders are squealing down the road, popping wheelies, flying around corners, and weaving in and out of traffic. There's a slang word for that brand of showoff—"squid"—and it's not an admirable term. Most sport-bike riders are sane, safe, and having a great time, and it's important to get those facts out to the media.

Motorcyclists have an undeserved reputation for being wild, fast, and reckless. It's our job to monitor and correct those stereotypes, setting the record straight and letting the public know that most motorcyclists care about safety and staying alive. If we are successful in this mission, people will not only see motorcycles differently, but they may even think about riding themselves. The reality is that

The Rolling Thunder ride is part of annual rally held over Memorial Day weekend as a tribute to American war heroes.

the more people who ride, or know people who ride, the safer it will become for all of us: as awareness grows, more people will be noticing bikes on the road.

Growing the sport of motorcycling is more than bringing in new riders. It's also about retaining them once they learn to ride and finding ways to keep them excited about all the ways they can stay engaged. For many, riding will be an end in and of itself, but, for others,

exploring all that the world of motorcycling has to offer will include developing new skills and building new friendships. It's also about working together with organizations and facilities you love to help them remain successful. I read an article in *Cycle World* about a racetrack that wanted to attract more riders, so they came up

Iron Butt Association members plan local events to introduce others to the sport.

with the idea of having small-group race clinics during times when the track was underutilized. Thus was born the Sunset Riders Clinic: they starting renting time slots for a lowered fee, bringing small groups of street riders onto the course at an affordable price, providing instruction, and letting them ride. As a direct result of creating new enthusiasts, attendance at the regular track days increased dramatically—a win-win for everyone.

The Iron Butt Association has encouraged members to sponsor local rallies, some as short as eight hours, to introduce the sport to those who might otherwise be intimidated by a longer, more competitive event. Once many riders get a taste for the fun of searching for specific locations, taking the required photos, and receiving scores, they're hooked. One Rallymaster created a five-month-long scavenger-style hunt that could be completed wherever the riders live and on their own time schedules. Riders uploaded all bonus photos with their smartphones and were usually scored within minutes, providing almost instant gratification. The Big Money Rally, as it is dubbed, is a great way to invite your friends to give rallying a try, and you can even tag along with them to score bonuses yourself.

Every style of riding has activities—whether on- or off-road, competitive or social—that welcome new attendees. If you have a specific interest, check it out and invite your friends. The thought of commuting in traffic to work every day on a bike might terrify one person, but that same person might light up when she thinks about being able to meander through the countryside, breathing in the fresh air and making stops off the beaten track to check out the work of local artisans. There may even come a time when you find yourself becoming bored with going on the same rides and routes with the same familiar faces. Take the time to explore new avenues for adventure. Try a dirt class, sign up for a tour of Africa or the Alps, or give the track a go. Bring along a friend who is feeling stale herself. You may both rekindle the excitement you had been lacking!

Supporting local brick-and-mortar businesses related to motorcycling is imperative if you want to ensure that they are there when you need to find just the right part or to try on a new pair of gloves. Shopping online may save you money, but using a local business as a fitting room while spending your dollars at the cheaper online store means that the neighborhood dealer won't be in business the next time you need them. Building relationships with service providers and dealerships and working together to create rider-friendly events creates a sense of community. Encourage your dealer to bring in speakers and offer workshops that will attract both new and experienced riders. One of our local dealers allows the Motorcycle Tourer's Forum (MTF) to use its parking lot as the starting point for their MTF SaddleSore, giving riders a safe place to gather at 5:00 in the morning to have their paperwork witnessed before they head out on their own. Another dealership sponsored an International Female Ride Day, turning over its entire parking lot to vendors catering to women motorcyclists.

What would you like to see more of? Perhaps educational events during the long winter months, such as workshops on routine bike maintenance that you can do at home? Are you willing to approach your dealer to see if they are interested in sponsoring such an event? If not, are you part of a group that might want to help, or are you creative enough to form a meet-up of like-minded women to pull off something of interest to a wider audience?

Would you like to be part of a group of women riders but haven't found the right one yet? Would you consider starting one of your own that you can tailor to meet your criteria? I went on a campout with a group of women who had formed only a year earlier, when a couple of friends decided that they wanted some other women with whom to ride. They were astonished at the turnout: more than fifty women came from not only the local area but also as far away as the neighboring state for a one-night event. Several of the attendees had started their own groups for similar reasons: they wanted to hang out with other riders and encourage them to keep bringing more women into the fold.

Motorcycling is too much fun to keep to yourself. I've seen women's faces light up with joy and excitement as they learn to ride, meet others who share their passion, and hang out together. I've witnessed women who were dusty and filthy from hours in the saddle, riding through everything Mother Nature can dish out, and loving every minute of it. I've spoken with young women just starting out and older women who have been riding for half a century. Girls who tagged along at the track with their fathers and brothers are now competing against them and winning. Mothers are getting on bikes and tackling tree roots, boulders, streams, and slippery hillsides, showing their daughters what they will be able to accomplish one day. The research supports the notion of a woman's sense of empowerment growing when she starts out on a motorcycle. Isn't that something worth sharing with every woman?

Acknowledgments

Voni Glaves, your support is beyond measure. Thanks for taking the time to offer insights and feedback.

David Hough, I appreciate your belief in my ability to communicate effectively.

To the many women (and a few men) who offered insights, shared anecdotes, raised good questions, suggested ideas, and gave generously of their support, I thank you: Lisa Hole; Laura Higgins; Anne Campbell; Kirsten and Jennifer Talken-Spaulding; Nancy Foote; Nancy Lefcourt; Pamela Ramsden; Molly Carbon; Lisa Sims; Rich O'Connor; Tyler Risk and Dangerous Curves; Hannah Starner; Kate Johnston; Joanne Donn and Gear Chic; Margaret Peart; Marsha Edie; Dave Biasotti; Brett Fladseth; Kelly, Jen, and Sabrina of Curve Unit; Amy Hunter; Annabelle Jiminez; Jeff and Cathy Earls; Heidi Still; Cierra Morris; Ruth Belcher; Lynne Downing; the Rainier Ravens; Deb Glasque and her blog, "The Fashionista Has an Iron Butt;" all of the attendees at the BMW-MOA Billings seminars and San Jose BMW's International Female Ride Day event; and my fellow women riders in the Iron Butt Association.

A huge thank you to all of the other unnamed women along the way who let me listen in while you opened up about your experiences, fears, successes, and love of riding.

Terry: Thanks for reintroducing me to the world of motorcycles and for bringing long-distance riding into our life together. It's been a wonderful adventure in every way.

Resources

Books

Code, Keith. *Twist of the Wrist Volume 2: The Basics of High-Performance Motorcycle Riding.* Los Angeles: California Superbike School, 1997

Hough, David. *More Proficient Motorcycling: Mastering the Ride.* Irvine, CA: Lumina Media, 2003.

————. *Proficient Motorcycling: The Ultimate Guide to Riding Well.* Irvine, CA: Lumina Media, 2000.

————. *Street Strategies: A Survival Guide for Motorcyclists.* Irvine, CA: Lumina Media, 2001.

Ienatsch, Nick. *Sport Riding Techniques: How to Develop Real World Skills for Speed, Safety, and Confidence on the Street and Track.* Phoenix, AZ: David Bull Publishing, 2003.

Parks, Lee. *Total Control: High-Performance Street Riding Techniques.* Motorbooks, 2003.

Websites

Events

International Female Ride Day
www.facebook.com/InternationalFemaleRideDay

Kyle Petty Charity Ride Across America
www.kylepettycharityride.org

Paul Pelland's Endless Road Tour
www.longhaulpaul.com

Speed Track Tales: A Welsh Perspective on the International Six Days Trials
www.speedtracktales.com

Sturgis Motorcycle Rally
www.sturgismotorcyclerally.com

X Games
xgames.espn.go.com

General Information

About Motorcycles
motorcycles.about.com

Auto Evolution's Motorcycling Pages
www.autoevolution.com/moto

AMA Motorcycle Museum Hall of Fame
www.motorcyclemuseum.org

American Motorcyclist Association (AMA)
www.americanmotorcyclist.com

CycleFish
www.cyclefish.com

Cycle World Magazine
www.cycleworld.com

FJR Motorcycle Forums
www.fjrforum.com

Insurance Institute for Highway Safety
www.iihs.org

JAFRUM Motorcycle Blog
blog.jafrum.com

Liz Jansen: Where the Road Meets Spirit
lizjansen.com

Mister Motorcycles
www.mistermotorcycles.com

Motorcycle Ergonomics Simulator
cycle-ergo.com

Motorcycle Consumer News
www.mcnews.com

Motorcycle Monster
www.motorcyclemonster.com

Motorcycle Roads
www.motorcycleroads.com

Motorcycle Sport Forums
www.motorcyclesport.net/forum

Motorcyclist Magazine
www.motorcyclistonline.com

Motoress
motoress.com

Ride Apart
rideapart.com

Ride Like a Pro: Motorcycle Instruction Courses and Videos
www.ridelikeapro.com

Silodrome Motorcycle Pages:
silodrome.com/category/motorcycles

Sound RIDER!
www.soundrider.com

Total Motorcycle
www.totalmotorcycle.com

The Vintagent (vintage motorcycles)
thevintagent.blogspot.com

Visordown (British online motorcycle community)
www.visordown.com

Women Riders Now
www.womenridersnow.com

Women's Coalition of Motorcyclists
www.wcm2020.org

Women's International Motorcycling Association
www.wimaworld.com

Shopping

Bike Bandit
www.bikebandit.com

K&N Performance Air Filters
www.knfilters.com

Motorcycle Gift Shop
www.motorcyclegiftshop.com

Motorcycle Superstore
www.motorcycle-superstore.com

Revzilla
www.revzilla.com

Touratech USA:
www.touratech-usa.com

Trip Planning

Best Biking Roads
www.bestbikingroads.com

Motorcycle Roads
www.motorcycleroads.com

MotoWhere?
www.motowhere.com

Open Road Journey
www.openroadjourney.com

Sunday Morning Rides
www.sundaymorningrides.com

Types of Riding

AMA Pro Racing
www.amaproracing.com

Canyonchasers Adventure, Sport, and Touring
www.canyonchasers.net

Edelweiss Bike Travel (touring)
Edelweissbike.com

Elena Myers (professional motorcycle racer)
elenamyers.com

Iron Butt Association
www.ironbutt.com

Jenny Tinmouth (British motorcycle racer)
www.jennytinmouth.com

Melissa Paris (professional road racer/motocross
   and flat track enthusiast)
melissaparis.com

Motorcycle Race Magazine
www.motorcycleracemag.com

Northeastern Motorcycle Tours
www.motorcycletours.com

Moto Magazine
www.motomagazine.co.uk

Moto USA
www.motorcycle-usa.com

Orange County Dualies (dual-sport riding)
www.dualies.com

RoadRUNNER Motorcycle Touring and Travel
roadrunner.travel

She'z Racing (Shelina Moreda, professional motorcycle racer):
shezracing.com

S.P. Rocket Girl
sprocketgirlracing.wordpress.com

Transworld Motocross
motocross.transworld.net

Women's Motocross Association (WMA)
www.womensmotocrossassociation.com

Index

Page numbers in **bold** typeface indicate a photograph.

Photos

Front cover: ssguy/Shutterstock; bikeriderlondon/Shutterstock; Dean Drobot/Shutterstock
Back cover: Wendy Crockett
Title page: Scott Smallin
Graphic elements: AKV/Shutterstock, Onchira Wongsiri/Shutterstock

Ted Alambaugh, 196; AlPavangkanan/Flickr, 61; Armyman/Flickr, 32; Arlington County/Flickr, 210; Mike Babiarz/Flickr, 148; Courtesy Ruth Belcher, 19, 190; blgrssby/Flickr, 59; Cori Chesnutt, 114 (right); Rusty Clark/Flickr, 121; Robert Couse-Baker/Flickr, 126; Steve Baker/Flickr, 209 (left), 225; dollars dollars, 181; Flattrackers and.../Flickr, 153; Corentin Foucaut/Flickr, 113 (right); Courtesy Connie Gabrick, 97; Courtesy Deb Gasque, 45, 184; Morgan Gilman Garritson, 13 (right), 168, 169; Paul Glaves, 27; Voni Glaves, 38, 51, 219; Dawn Hein, 202; Craig Howell, 120; kazamatsuri/Flickr, 123; Andy Kirby, 4; Dustin Knudsen, 128; Jenny Lundquist/Flickr, 186, 240; Courtesy Lynda Lahman, 33, 49, 212; Courtesy Jodie Lawrosky, 42, 76, 98, 122, 129; Anthony Mills, 40, 50, 62, 67, 86, 165, 188; North Carolina National Guard/Flickr; Anthony Osbourne, 48; PublicAffairsOfficeFortWainwright/ Flickr, 68; Dace Raven, 166; Joe Ross/Flickr, 91; Dave S, 197; Bob Scott, 159; Shakenaw America/ Flickr, 215; David Sifry/Flickr, 127; Scott Smallin, 8, 108; Bill Smith/Flickr, 141; Tobie Stevens, 6, 31, 35, 37, 47, 78, 132, 162, 178, 179, 191, 192, 193, 201, 203–205, 220, 221; MikeT/Flickr, 119; USAGLivornoPAO/Flickr, 54; versageek/Flickr, 101; Videowokart/Flickr, 102; courtesy Cletha Walstrom, 21, 104, 124; Lumen Photos/Shutterstock, 135 ; Shutterstock, 230

Shutterstock: A.B.G, 13, (left); kong act, 95; apiguide, 64; Andrey Armyagov, 28, 30, 44; David Arts, 222; Philip Arno Photography, 17; BallBall14, 75; Darin Bergquist, 214; BestPhotoStudio, 131; Bhakpong, 177; bibiphoto, 7, 160; Barry Blackburn, 11 (center), 209 (right); bluehand, 136 (bottom); bopra77, 115 (right); buydeephoto, 155 (top); Dmitry ND, 72; Elena Elisseeva, 117; ermess, 52, 70, 116 (right); Ramon Espelt Photography, 2-3, 84; Geza Farkas, 36, 69; Sanit Fuangnakhon, 133; FotograFFF, 116 (left); Rodrigo Garrido, 194; goodluz, 144; Len Green, 111 (left); Adam Gregor, 66, 83; Supanee Hickman, 12; Brendan Howard, 11 (top); il4lcocl2, 18; Evgenii Iaroshevskii, 23; EvrenKalinbacak, 114 (left); KarSol, 110; KAZLOVA IRYNA, 20; Sergey Kohl, 15, 41, 112 (right); Krasnopolski, 74; TK Kurikawa, 115 (left); Laborant, 151 (top); LianeM, 88; Luis Louro, 56; Izabela Magier, 130, 146; Gabriele Maltinti, 10, 175; Igor Matic, 16; Tyler McKay, 158; mikeledray, 145; Monkey Business Images, 79; Oleg Moskaliuk, 96; Mariusz Niedzwiedzki, 200; Alexandru Nika, 156 (bottom); Nikkolia, 77; Viacheslav Nikolaenko, 112 (left); Octopus, 149; Guillermo Olaizola, 227; Anna Omelchenko, 170; PANIGALE, 111 (right); paperbees, 137; Pavel L Phtot and Vidoe; Raquel Pedrosa, 81; Noel Pennington, 211; anuruk perai, 152; PHILIPIMAGE, 125; Niran Phonruang, 155 (bottom); Radule, 136 (top); Chuck Rausin, 132; Rocksweeper, 187; betto rodrigues, 142, 156 (top); Denys Sapozhnik, 71; Eugene Sergeev, 113 (left); L. Siekierski, 14; Joseph Sohm, 89; Sonrak, 24; tarapong srichaiyos, 176; Wally Stemberger, 11 (bottom); Suvorov_Alex, 198; Tamisclao, 154; Tapat.p, 80; TonyV3112, 140; trekandshoot, 25; Mike Vande Ven Jr, 106; victorass, 174; Evgeny Vorobyev, 223; vtwinpixel, 99; Chuck Wagner, 93; weltreisendertj, 90; Chamille White, 150; Steiner Wolfgang, 92, 139, 173, 216; Jimmy Yan, 151 (bottom)

About the Author

Lynda Lahman is the only person to complete the eleven-day Iron Butt Rally as a pillion (twice) and as a rider. She writes a regular column, *Perspective*, for *Iron Butt Magazine*, a publication dedicated to safe long-distance motorcycling, and is the author of three other books: *The Winner's Mind: Strengthening Mental Skills in Athletes*, *Two-Up: Navigating a Relationship 1,000 Miles at a Time*, and *From Iron Lung to Iron Butt: Riding Polio into History*.

Lynda has a private practice as a mental skills coach (www.thewinnersmind.com), helping athletes break through mental barriers to reach peak performance. She lives with her husband, Terry, in Washington.